THE FIRST AND SECOND
EPISTLES TO THE THESSALONIANS

NEW TESTAMENT FOR SPIRITUAL READING

VOLUME 18

Edited by

John L. McKenzie, S.J.

THE FIRST EPISTLE
TO THE THESSALONIANS

HEINZ SCHÜRMANN

THE SECOND EPISTLE
TO THE THESSALONIANS

HANS-ANDREAS EGENOLF

CROSSROAD • NEW YORK

2585

1981
The Crossroad Publishing Company
575 Lexington Avenue, New York, NY 10022

Originally published as *Der erste Brief an die Thessalonicher* and
Der zweite Brief an die Thessalonicher
© 1962, 1965 by Patmos-Verlag
from the series *Geistliche Schriftlesung*
edited by Wolfgang Trilling
with Karl Hermann Schelke and Heinz Schürmann

English translation © 1969 by Burns & Oates, Limited, London
Translated by William Glen-Doepel

Library of Congress Catalog Card Number: 81-68173
ISBN: 0-8245-0127-6

PREFACE

First Thessalonians has a unique interest; it is the first of the extant letters of Paul to be written. If Second Thessalonians is also the work of Paul (which is questioned by some modern scholars) it must follow the first by no more than a few weeks. The two letters taken together permit us to study one of the more important and pressing problems of the early church which has ceased to be a problem in the contemporary church. Yet our own attitude towards the problem may mean that we still have the problem, but view it in another way.

The two letters, to which some other New Testament passages can be added, show clearly that many in the early church, if not most, believed that the Second Coming of Jesus could be expected within the span of a normal lifetime. The language of Paul, if it is studied without prejudice, indicates that he himself shared this belief; and no question would ever have been raised about his language if it had not been feared that the obvious interpretation of Paul would admit error in the inspired and infallible books of the New Testament. We now know that the personal opinions of Paul, whether about the time of the Second Coming or about the conformation of the visible universe, have nothing to do with the inspiration and the infallibility of the New Testament. We also know that Paul, like other biblical writers, thought and spoke in the patterns of thought and speech of the world in which he lived.

The somewhat different responses to the problem in the two letters have been alleged among the reasons for doubting that Paul is the author of Second Thessalonians. The first epistle, especially in 4:14–18, leaves little doubt that the author expects himself and his contemporaries to experience the Second Coming. The problem of what is to happen to those who are still alive at the time of the Second Coming is not a live problem either in modern scholarship or in popular belief. It is exactly this implication which is rejected in Second Thessalonians 2:1–12. Yet this ambiguity is not a certain indication that Paul is not the author of both letters. Belief in the Second Coming cannot escape ambiguity, for it does not permit the believer to affirm anything about the date. The believer must act as if it were both near and remote. But the language in which Paul corrects his own ambiguity is not altogether satisfactory; so much must be conceded to the doubt.

The thrust of both letters, however, is that the time of the Second Coming has nothing to do with the character of the Christian life. Whether the Second Coming is near or remote, it absolves no one of his Christian responsibilities. Therefore both letters contain admonitions to the practical execution of the Christian moral mandate without reference to the Second Coming. These admonitions become a standard feature in the later epistles of Paul, in most of which there is no explicit consideration of the Second Coming. They present an ideal of the Christian life, as Dr. Schürmann points out, to be lived in the *diaspora,* by a small Christian minority in a pagan world. The life of the Christian community in such a situation is itself the proclamation of the gospel to the pagan world.

The moral ideal of the epistles is the very antithesis of the " flight from the world " which has been so often proposed as genuine evangelical Christianity. In practice it has meant either the isolation of the Christian minority from the defilement of the world or the creation of a Christian majority in which the Christian life, it is assumed, becomes the norm of the community. In the first of these cases the community renounces any

effort to proclaim the gospel to the non-Christian world in which
it lives. It has no message for that world, and it does not manifest the saving love of Christ. In the second case the Christian
life which becomes the norm has been an enfeebled form of
Christianity. Medieval Europe had a massive Christian majority,
but it was in no way an example of the Christian ideal. The
church has rarely realized itself as Paul expected the church of
Thessalonica to realize itself. In our own day it was not until the
Second Vatican Council that the church began to think of itself
as the missionary church of the *diaspora*, the phrase recently
restored to circulation by Karl Rahner. If it is to be this missionary church, it will have to think of itself as proclaiming the
gospel by the life of its members.

I have suggested that the problem of the Second Coming may
still be with us under another form; and it must be admitted
that Paul does not speak directly to our problem. The church of
Thessalonica, like some other early churches, was weakened in
its faith and in its works because it was excessively eschatological;
not all Christian problems of belief and conduct are solved by an
immediate reference to the Second Coming. Our problem is that
we are scarcely eschatological at all. Our problems are seen as
problems which can be and must be resolved within human
experience. Christian eschatological belief, if it affirms anything,
affirms that the basic human problems are not soluble within
human experience but only by the act of God in Christ. Many
of our contemporaries find it difficult to reconcile even the mini-
mum of eschatological belief with the theology of the secular
city. Up to this writing no genius has arisen who has synthesized
both the eschatological faith and the mandate of the church to
aid its fellow men by the works of love.

If the problem is put in these terms, it may not be so insoluble.
Both the eschatological faith and the mandate are clear in the
New Testament. The Christian is humble enough to know that

his own works of love will not ultimately solve the basic problems of humanity (nor indeed will the collective love of the church). He is saddened because the collective love of the church has never approached its full potential; and he has no idea what might have been done about the basic problems of humanity if the potential had been reached. He is quite sure that he cannot maintain his eschatological faith by abandoning the mandate for such substitutes as ghetto Christianity or Christian imperialism.

If the basic problems of mankind are soluble only by the saving act of God in Christ, the Christian must remember that the saving act is begun with the incarnation and continued in the church. The saving act is not restricted to the Second Coming. There is a sense in which the church is the Second Coming; indeed, the church has to think in these terms if it is to fulfill its mandate. It is the claim of the church that no one experiences the saving act of Christ except in and through the church. Critics of the church have pointed out with justice that members and unbelievers have not often experienced in and through the church that love which attends to their basic human needs such as food, clothing and shelter. It has presented an eschatological solution of the basic human problems in a world which is not the *eschaton* and with which the church does not deal as if it were the *eschaton*. If one does not think eschatologically one has to think in purely secular terms; there seems to be no other choice. And since the church has refused to think consistently eschatologically, it has thought in purely secular terms most of the time. The paradox of the matter is that one cannot grip the basic human problems unless one thinks eschatologically. Paul did not speak directly to our problems, but he thought eschatologically. We have not improved on his presentation of Christian life in the *diaspora*.

JOHN L. McKENZIE, S.J.

The First Epistle
to the Thessalonians

INTRODUCTION

1. For whom did the apostle Paul write the First Epistle to the Thessalonians? In the first place, for a small diaspora community that had not yet settled down and was in peril and oppressed, the church in Thessalonica (present-day Salonika in Macedonia), in the autumn of A.D. 51. But our epistle is a letter by an apostle. An apostolic letter has a fundamental importance for the whole church and for the life of the church in all ages. As such it is the word of God. But the First Epistle to the Thessalonians is the word of God in a quite special way for those Christian communities that have to live in a non-Christian environment. The early church consisted of small fraternal communities in the midst of a pagan environment, scattered over the world among all peoples and nations, without external power, in poverty and weakness, but full of inner glory. Our epistle has something to say to such communities, whether of the past, present, or future. It is intended for Christians in unfortunate circumstances, for a church that (a) as a new foundation is still small and unstable, (b) is endangered by an environment that lives differently, and (c) suffers persecution because of its faith.

(a) The church in Thessalonica was a small and still unstable community which had been founded only a few months before (perhaps in the spring of A.D. 51). About fifteen years after his call on the road to Damascus (about A.D. 34), Paul had set out with Silvanus on a wide incursion into pagan territory in the attempt to build up a third great string of missions, that of Asia

Minor and Europe, with Ephesus as the later center (cf. Acts 15 : 36—18 : 22).

Coming from Philippi, Paul and Silvanus, with their assistant Timothy, had been able to lay the foundations of a community in Thessalonica: a few Jews, but also a large number of pagans who, as God-fearing men, used to attend the Jewish assemblies in the synagogue (Acts 17 : 2ff.), had come to the faith (1 : 6ff.) and been converted (1 : 9). But the community lacked what is so often missing in the cases of our diaspora communities also: solid, constructive teaching, a training in faith of those who have found their way to a convinced and personal faith. This kind of conversion and finding of faith must be worked on and strengthened by pastoral help. This pastoral work of Paul and Silvanus, however (cf. 2 : 7–12), had been abruptly broken off in Thessalonica when those Jews who had remained unconverted succeeded in rousing the population and authorities of the town against the missionaries. The latter were forced to leave the town by night (Acts 17 : 5–10), and had since had no opportunity of returning (2 : 18; 3 : 6). Thus Paul was seriously concerned about the community, and even feared that the young foundation might have been destroyed in the months since his departure (3 : 5–8). His worries about the community troubled him so much that he felt he " could bear it no longer " (3 : 1). To have to live with such care was no longer a bearable life (3 : 8). Paul knows how much there " is lacking " in the newly-won Christians that he must supply (3 : 10), and how much " establishing " the new-found faith required (3 : 2), how much it needed the grace of persistence (5 : 23f.). Thus he writes his letter in great pastoral care to a community that is not yet fully established and settled.

(b) The storms of the times caused men to move about a lot at that period. World-wide trade and a strange unrest contributed

towards making men unstable and rootless. Thus it happened
that soon, in towns both large and small, there were small communities of Christians in the midst of a pagan environment. But
men "who do not know God" (4:5) necessarily live according
to other laws than Christians, who have "turned to God from
idols to serve a living and true God" (1:9). The fundamental
command to the newly converted Christian in his pagan and
immoral environment must be: be different! Paul knows that
the Christian remains in peril after his conversion and baptism.
Left without help, he is always in danger of falling back into his
old life before conversion, into the habits of his milieu. He needs
special strengthening from the Lord (3:12f.), "preservation" by
God (5:23f.) if he is not to succumb to these temptations. The
typical vices of the ancient pagan world, sexual immorality and
dishonesty, remained dangers for the newly converted Christians,
against which it was also necessary to warn them (4:3–8), as
Paul saw quite plainly. Indeed, the environment can so corrupt
the Christian conscience that the sixth and seventh commandments can even be "disregarded" as no longer binding (4:8),
so that even the fundamental principles can be shaken. Obviously, Paul had reason to issue this warning. In Thessalonica
there were also members of the brethren who were shy of work
and preferred to stand talking in the marketplace rather than
order their personal and domestic life (4:11ff.; 2 Thess. 3:6–15).
There are people in the community who live wrongly (5:14)
and must be constantly admonished, also "weak" brethren
(5:14) who need constant instruction and support, the "fainthearted" (5:4) and those who "grieve" (4:13.18; 5:11), who
needed to be raised up. Paul also takes note of envy (5:12),
injustice and unkindness (5:15), and failures to love (3:12). He
knows that a diaspora community has its moral shortcomings

(3:10) and is not perfect (3:12; 4:10; 5:23). Christians are still human, and diaspora Christians are always at risk. We should not idealize the church of Thessalonica if we want to understand the warnings of Paul. These Christians are like us in many respects—in their susceptibility, weakness, and peril.

(c) Paul also knows that the community is being persecuted. This was its fate from the beginning (1:6; cf. Acts 17:5–10), and it was to remain like that after the flight of the missionaries (2:14; 2 Thess. 1:4). This is the fate of the church from the beginning in this world (2:14). Paul sees these oppressions as a divine necessity. It is the lot of the Christians in the last times (3:3f.). But behind these oppressions stands Satan as their real originator (3:5; cf. 2:18). That is why Paul is worried about the existence of the community (3:5.8) and concerned that it be established (3:13) and preserved (5:23). These oppressions could be a real temptation for the community (3:5). A community under pressure is always a community in peril.

2. A diaspora community—unsettled, in danger, and oppressed, without apostolic pastoral care—what help is there for it? Paul expects a strengthening of the community's faith from God alone who will perfect the work (5:24) that he began when he called them to be Christians (1:4; 4:7; 5:24), from God (4:9) and from Christ, who will cause brotherly love to grow in the community (3:12f.), and also from the Holy Spirit, who keeps hope alive in the community (5:19ff.), and does the work of sanctification (4:8; 5:23; 2 Thess. 2:13). What God achieves in the community through grace can be briefly summed up as faith, love, and hope. These are what can keep the poor, endangered, and oppressed community alive (1:3; 5:8; cf. 3:6). Paul, as a pastor, looks at what constitutes the substance of a community. He emphasizes what is important.

(a) Being a Christian means, briefly, having faith (cf. 3:5. 7f. 10). Faith must always be named first when the good points of a community are listed (1:3; 3:6). But what is the faith that overcomes all obstacles and causes a weak community " to stand fast " (3:8)?

Paul is thinking of a faith that comprises conversion " to God from idols " (1:9). No one becomes a Christian in the full sense if he does not turn in faith to God and away from sin: " He who believes and is baptized will be saved," says the resurrected Christ (Mk. 16:16). And Peter says the same thing in his sermon at the first Pentecost: " Repent, and be baptized every one of you in the name of Jesus Christ for the forgiveness of your sins; and [then] you shall receive the gift of the Holy Spirit " (Acts 2:38). This faith, that includes a true conversion, has in life the form of service, the " conversion " is preserved in a service of God (1:9), which embraces the whole of life. This is ultimately because faith in its full form already contains love. Thus it can be almost equated with love (cf. 3:10.12), and both have always to be mentioned close together (3:6). But a loving faith is like a " breastplate " (5:8).

Paul conceives of faith as something dynamic, always at work (1:3). Obviously, he is thinking of a strength of faith that is given by the Holy Spirit, that is pneumatic in nature (cf. 1 Cor. 12:9). A faith that is inspired by the Spirit can " remove mountains " (1 Cor. 13:2) and make the impossible possible: " And these signs will accompany those who believe: in my name they will cast out demons; they will speak in new tongues; they will pick up serpents, and if they drink any deadly thing, it will not hurt them; they will lay their hands on the sick, and they will recover " (Mk. 16:17f.). Paul is thinking of a faith that expresses itself in spiritual service (5:19–22). There is a faith that makes one " aglow with the Spirit " (Rom. 12:11). Such a faith that leads one to serve in the Spirit builds up community (cf. 5:12f.) and overcomes all obstacles. With this kind of faith one is " in the Holy Spirit and with full conviction " (1:5). This kind of faith is full of enthusiasm and the " joy inspired by the Holy Spirit " (1:6), a joy that sounds forth its song and attracts others (1:8).

The most effective aid to faith is the word that is of the Spirit. Filled with the Spirit (1:5; 2:1) it is able to arouse faith and build up the community (2:7–12; 3:10; 5:12f.). With its inner strength it has an effect on the hearts of the faithful (2:13a). It is able to strengthen the weak and vacillating (3:2; 5:14) and comfort the fainthearted (3:2; 4:18; 5:11.14). Above all it is the word of faith, mighty in the Spirit, that is able to give support and steadfastness to weak and endangered communities.

In Paul himself one can admire the degree to which such a living faith is also " seeing." He sees all things and events in the light of God. The eyes of this kind of faith are clairvoyant. In this light he is able to see what glory surrounds even the poorest little diaspora community which is there " in God the Father and the Lord Jesus Christ " and represents the church, the elected people of God of the last times (1:1). Faith is able to look behind the curtain and does not let smallness and weakness blind one to the glory of the works of God. With these eyes one can see the brethren as " beloved by God " (1:4), " chosen ones " (1:4), ones who are " called " (2:12; 5:24). Under the sun of these eyes of faith all ill-humor vanishes. These eyes also know about the struggle between God and Satan. Whoever does not see Satan is foolish and does not properly understand. It is he who is behind all persecutions (2:18; 3:5). But faith knows that God is stronger than Satan

(3:11) and his anti-Christian helpers (2 Thess. 2:3.8); he sees God, Christ, and the Holy Spirit powerfully at work within the community. It is God who has chosen the faithful from eternity (1:4) and called them to be Christians (1:4; 4:7; 5:24), to his glorious kingdom (2:12). God himself is at work in his word (2:13; 4:9). He sanctifies the faithful and preserves them (5:23) by giving the Holy Spirit (4:8; 5:23; 2 Thess. 2:13). He will also perfect (5:24) what he has begun. All perfection in the community, all growth in love comes from the Lord (3:12), who strengthens us and gives us the grace of persistence (3:13). And the Holy Spirit is at work in the service of him and the gifts of grace (5:19–22). Thus the community, in all its wretchedness, openness to temptation, and the wiles of Satan, is entirely held and worked through by the action of the grace of God and Christ in the Holy Spirit. Whoever could see a community with the eyes of faith that Paul had would be preserved from all despondency; it would be the end of his faintheartedness.

(b) The great support of a diaspora community is brotherly love. Brotherly love is the subject in which it is primarily God, as the "inner teacher," who instructs the faithful in their hearts (4:9). It is the principle of unity and order in the community. It is concerned everywhere to create unity. It orders the relationship of the members of the community to their superiors and also among one another (5:12ff.). It is also the bond between the apostle and his community (3:6.12). It is the power that imposes on those whose lives are disorderly the discipline of penance and overcomes sin, raises up the fainthearted, supports the weak, makes long-suffering, and conquers injustice through good deeds (5:14f.). Love makes one capable of the laborious toil (1:3) that keeps the life of the community going (5:12).

Brotherly love in the community overflows and is directed towards all the brethren in the faith (4:10). Thus it helps to preserve the church unity between the communities and individual Christians in the diaspora. But it does not exclude those who do not believe (3:12; 5:15). This is the kind of love that strengthens hearts. In it, ultimately, all holiness is contained and made sure (3:13). Thus a diaspora community will also have to be a brotherhood, or else it will soon stop being a Christian community.

(c) An especially strong force in an oppressed community is hope (1:3; 2:19; 4:13; 5:8). But Paul sees it as a living "waiting for" the Lord (1:10). To wait for the Lord is to wait in love. The Lord is longed for passionately: to be able to be "with the Lord" is the epitomy of all bliss (4:14.17; 5:10). But when someone wants something he likes to believe in it. Whoever longs lovingly for the Lord to come hopes that he is near, counts on his proximity. Behind the early Christian's expectation that Christ would return soon there was much love. But this expectation in the early church was not only the expression of a wish; it could point to clear signs. There were two experiences of faith in particular which made the end appear "near."

First, faith sees that the Lord, whose coming we are waiting for, has already risen from the grave, as the "first-born from the dead" (Col. 1:18). The resurrection is the beginning of the end. With it the future has already begun. The light of the Last Judgment is already visible (5:4), the faithful already belong to the "day," the "light" (5:5.8). The expectation of the early Christians derives, therefore, from its fulfillment, in the resurrection of Jesus (1:10; 4:14; 5:10). A community that believes in the resurrection of Jesus knows that the end has quite literally come "near," is in fact pressing close upon them. But if God has already begun his last great deed, then he will also complete it soon. The new age of the world has begun with the resurrection of Jesus. What already exists and is essentially near can no longer be easily thought of as being a long way off in time.

A persecuted community, however, experiences the proximity of the end in another way: from the suffering that it is undergoing (1:6; 2:14; 3:3ff.; 2 Thess. 1:4), for this is a sign of the end (3:4; 2:14ff.), "for the time has come for judgment to begin with the household of God" (1 Pet. 4:17). Paul knows that the wrath of God's judgment has already begun (2:16). Thus an actual eschatological persecution teaches people to look out for the approach of the Lord (1:3), who will "deliver us from the wrath to come" (1:10; cf. 5:9; 2 Thess. 1:10). Paul sees the persecution to which he and the community are subjected in the light of the morals of the Lord as the promised great "tribulation" (Mk. 13:24) which is to come before the end. In this kind of suffering Christians have always the particular nearness of the Lord. This nearness is certainly not meant only as a nearness in time, though it is that also. For Christ will break into time and is already constantly shining into history from beyond all time and history. From his eternity, from beyond the grave, he is "near" every moment of passing time between his ascension and his parousia. This nearness increases, however, in the measure that the suffering of the last times increases. Times of persecution bring one close to Christ in a special way, and in them the Lord is particularly "near" to his people with grace, help, and promise. Thus the first martyr of the church was able to give the valid testimony: "Behold, I see the heavens opened, and the Son of man standing at the right hand of God " (Acts 7:56). In this particular kind of grace Christ is not equally " close " to every age. It is times of persecution that have a particular right to testify to the nearness of the Lord. Thus the testimony of Paul in both of the Epistles to the Thessalonians is a prophetic testimony from the experience of persecution. It is the testimony of a man filled with the Spirit who, undergoing martyrdom, sees " the heavens open " and the Lord " near."

It is true that the nearness of the Lord is understood by Paul also in terms of time. The possibility that the Lord is coming soon requires above all " constant readiness," for " of that day or that hour no one knows " (Mk. 13:32). The basic demand is for watchful and sober readiness (5:1-11). At the arrival of the Lord everyone must be able to stand " blameless " before him (3:13; 5:23). Thus such an expectation is a mighty spur to " constant readiness." An expectation of Christ's imminent arrival that imagines that it has certain knowledge of the approaching end (2 Thess. 2:1f.) is not compatible with the uncertainty of the hour. No, no one is certain. But love is not to be blamed if it not only knows that the beloved and longingly awaited Lord is not only actually " near," but hopes and wishes beyond that and even thinks in loving longing that he might perhaps even come in our lifetime (cf. esp. 4:15.17).

All salvation is to be expected from the coming Lord. The parousia is a great feast of victory for Christians (4:13-18; 2:19f.; 5:9ff.). Then all loving hope is realized: we shall be " with the Lord " (4:14.17; 5:10). But where this kind of hope is alive, the life of the community gains great strength, much " comfort " (4:13.18; 5:11), and above all an endurance in all suffering that overcomes the world (1:3).

OUTLINE

The Close of the Letter (5:25–28)
THE CLOSE OF THE LETTER (5:25–28)

I. A request to be remembered in prayer (5:25)

II. Intended for the whole community (5:26–27)

III. Blessing (5:28)

THE OPENING OF THE LETTER (1:1)

THE LETTERHEAD (1:1)

The Senders and the Addressee (1:1a)

¹ᵃ *Paul, Silvanus, and Timothy* . . .

Paul, Silvanus, and Timothy are writing this letter together. The Lord had sent out his apostles (Mk. 6:7) and disciples (Lk. 10:1) in twos, because, according to Old Testament law (Deut. 19:13), a truth had to be testified to by two or three witnesses. A letter sent by three people, and is thus attested several times, is an official document: something is to be communicated to us officially by God, the contents of which is solemnly attested. This enjoins us to pay careful attention; we cannot read the letter without feeling involved.

Who is talking to us in it? Primarily, the apostle Paul. At Damascus he had received his revelation and his mission directly from the Lord. Thinking of this he is able to write: "For what we preach is not ourselves, but Jesus Christ as Lord, with ourselves as your servants for Jesus' sake. For it is the God who said: 'Let light shine out of darkness,' who has shone in our hearts to give the light of the knowledge of the glory of God in the faith of Christ " (2 Cor. 4:5–6). On that occasion it was like the day when God created light (Gen. 1:3). Paul speaks out of this light of revelation; it shines out of all his words.

How can we understand what he is saying? Only if the same

3

light of God illuminates us also. Light comes from the word of God. God speaks to us primarily through the luminous preaching of the church; but he also talks directly to us in our hearts through the Holy Spirit, through his inner light that seeks to illuminate all the truth of faith from within. God speaks both outwardly and inwardly: we cannot understand what is spoken out of the light of God's revelation if the same light of God does not light it up within us.

Paul took Silvanus with him on his great missionary journey. Why did he do that? Paul had not seen the miracles of the Lord, nor listened to his words. Above all, he was not able, like the first apostles, to testify as an eye-witness to the resurrection on the third day. Therefore, he had to seek connection with Peter and the other first disciples of the Lord and take over what they handed on. Silvanus, however, was able to give an excellent testimony to this earliest tradition of the church, for he had once belonged to the leaders of the original church in Jerusalem, had enjoyed the special trust of the twelve, and was one of the early Christian prophets. He was also particularly suited to teach and instruct. Now we know that what Silvanus tells us comes from the earliest tradition of the church, has the testimony of the first apostles, the college of the twelve, behind it, and connects us with Jesus himself. The letter places our faith on the apostolic foundation on which the church is built. Moreover, the gospel of faith comes to us from the primary source.

The two missionaries place their faithful "helper" (Acts 19:22), Timothy, beside themselves in a very fraternal spirit. An untroubled affection exists between the three senders of the letter, and also between them and the community. Here Paul can dispense with his title of apostle; he does not especially need to emphasize his apostolic authority to the Thessalonians. Only in the order of the names is there a gentle indication of the very different positions of the three men. Where there is brotherly love, there is no need for much to be made of position and authority. It is only when quarrels or false teachings call authority into question that it must be emphasized. Offices and functions in the church have the form of services, according to the rule of the Lord: " If any one would be first, he must be last of all and servant of all " (Mk. 9:35).

1a. . . To the church of the Thessalonians in God the Father and the Lord Jesus Christ :

A tiny church community has existed for a few months among the inhabitants of Thessalonica, and to outward appearances it certainly still seems weak and pitiful. But in Paul's eyes it is great. This kind of community has high dignity; it is something quite different from a civic community in a particular place. This must be clearly stated: it is in God the Father and the Lord Jesus Christ. This is what gives it its exalted position. It stands in a special relation to God, the Father of Jesus Christ, who is the Father of us all. And it stands in a special relation to Jesus Christ, who was raised after his resurrection to the throne of heaven and is now Lord over the church and the whole cosmos. A Christian community owes its existence and its continuance always to this Father and this Lord of glory. It is they who are building it up from heaven. This gives it the closest possible relation to God the Father and the Lord Jesus Christ; it belongs to them. A Christian knows what high dignity even the most insignificant looking community possesses, and what an honor it is to be allowed to belong to it.

The Greek word for community is " *ekklesia,*" which means basically " church," but often also the " community," and sometimes also the " community assembly." How can the Greek word have three different meanings? Well, wherever a " community " is formed, there " church " is brought into existence. A community is the church on a small scale. But community comes about by Christian " gatherings," especially when they also " gather " themselves inwardly in their common brotherhood in the liturgy of the word and the celebration of the Eucharist. In this assembly God is gathering his " church," the people of the last times, called together out of all the peoples. Thus the church is a holy " gathering of God." This always becomes apparent when a community assembles.

Where can we experience the presence of Christ? Certainly, in a special way, at the Eucharist, but also when the word of Christ is read; and also when two or three are " gathered " in his name (Mt. 18:20) and are one amongst themselves. This is the reason that it is so important that Christians gather wherever they can: " And let us consider how to stir up one another to love and good works, not neglecting to meet together . . . , but encouraging one another, and all the more as you see the Day [of the Lord] drawing near " (Heb. 10:24f.).

When he was dictating this letter, Paul had in mind this community gathered to celebrate the Lord's Supper, the meal of love. He sees each member individually before him, but he also sees them as an assembled community, as the church. However much the word of God speaks to the individual, it always speaks to him as a member of the community. We too shall understand these words better when we see ourselves as members of the community, as brothers within a brotherhood; for love teaches understanding.

The Greeting (1:1b)

¹ᵇGrace to you and peace.

To the Thessalonians the wish " grace to you and peace " must
have sounded unusual and strange, and we too should sit up
and take notice. Greeks generally greeted one another with the
invitation to " joy " and Jews wished one another " peace."
But what are Christians to wish one another? Paul is seeking
for new words. Love calls one to concentrate on essentials; that
is why he wishes what seems the most important thing to him:
the grace of God and peace with God. " Grace to you and peace
from God the Father and the Lord Jesus Christ ": this is the
greeting that Paul will go on to write in all his later letters
(cf. 2 Thess. 1:2).

Thus Paul wishes the grace and peace that come from God and
from Christ. God is telling us here that he wants to be gracious
towards us and that he has made peace with us. This is the
theme that underlies everything that the letter says. It is a joyous
message of salvation, therefore, that the emissaries of God are
bringing us. If we see all the statements of the letter as a message
of salvation that comes from God, then we have properly understood them.

This greeting that brings in God is certainly not an empty
one. We recall that the Lord said about the disciples' greeting:
" Whatever house you enter, first say, ' peace be to this house!'
And if a son of peace is there, your peace shall rest upon him;
but if not it shall return to you " (Lk. 10:5f.). Christians know
that their greeting is effective, that it is not just a polite saluta-
tion. Their greeting is a prayer to which God gives power; thus

they are able to greet one another in a way that the greeting takes effect.

Our letter was written more than nineteen hundred years ago to the Christians in Thessalonica. Does it still have anything to say to us today? Even in the earliest times the apostolic communities knew that a letter from an apostle was never written simply to a single community, but was intended also to be passed on to other communities. These too were supposed—in different circumstances and perhaps in a different way—to learn from it. Thus we find Paul himself writing to the Colossians: "And when this letter has been read among you, have it read also in a church of the Laodiceans; and see that you read also the letter from Laodicea" (Col. 4:16). What is the inner reason for the general validity of the apostolic letters? They are written to communities which represent the church. Thus they are valid for other communities, even for those of today, in which the same church lives on. Thus we are all addressed. The grace and the peace that the Apostle wants to communicate to his listeners and readers is also intended for us. That is why we still have to ask what the letter has to tell us here and now, in our own day.

THE BODY OF THE LETTER
(1:2—5:24)

AFFECTIONATE MEMORIES (1:2–3:13)

Paul's epistles are apostolic pastoral letters. They are intended to teach and exhort, thus firmly establishing the community. Paul is always a preacher, whether he is speaking or writing. Like most sermons, his letters are also generally divided into two parts. First Paul reminds us of what God has done, his saving activity; then he goes on to draw out, in a second part, the consequences for Christian life. Christian life is basically the grateful remembrance of God's saving work, but also the loving effort to live a life pleasing to God (4:1). So, in the First Epistle to the Thessalonians, Paul engages with the community in thoughtful reflection: in a fundamental discussion (Part I) he reminds the community of the great things that God has done for it (1:2—3:13) when he elected and called it. In Part II (4:1—5:24) he goes on to say what God wants from it and the way that Christians should live in the community: "Lead a life worthy of God, who calls you into his own kingdom and glory" (2:12)—in reverse order, that could be a comprehensive title for both parts of the letter.

As a rule Paul begins his letters, as here, with a statement of great thanksgiving to God, much broader and deeper than was customary in the expressions of gratitude in letters of the time. In our letter, however, Paul is so "abounding in thanksgiving" (Col. 2:7) that the introductory expression of thanks goes through and frames the whole first part of the letter (1:2—3:13).

Introductory Thanksgiving (1:2–3)

[2] *We give thanks to God always for you all, constantly mentioning you in our prayers, . . .*

Paul uses prayer in his missionary work; he regularly includes the concerns of his communities in his apostolic prayer of intercession, but his remembrance then always automatically becomes a thanksgiving. This is what happens with someone who sees with clear eyes God working in communities and souls. Obviously, Paul sees the working of God's grace more clearly than the shortcomings that he has to mention in his prayer of intercession. It is shortsighted to see only the inadequacies; this is the way blind men behave, in whom " the God of this world has blinded the minds . . . , to keep them from seeing the light of the gospel " (2 Cor. 4:4).

The thanksgiving of the Christian is broad and deep, all-embracing in terms of space and time. He accepts thankfully the working of God's grace in all its breadth: " Give thanks in all circumstances; for this is the will of God in Christ Jesus for you " (5:18). Absolutely everything must be carried back to God and transformed into thanksgiving, " so that as grace extends to more and more people it may increase thanksgiving, to the glory of God " (2 Cor. 4:15). This thanksgiving is never ending: " Always and for everything giving thanks " (Eph. 5:20). This sacrificial fire of universal and constant thanksgiving can only be ignited in the hearts of the faithful by the Holy Spirit. But we should know that this fire has already been lit in us and therefore the great thanksgiving made possible for us also. It is the manner of the heathen not to " honor him as God or give thanks to him " (Rom. 1:21).

The gratitude of Christians has its climax in the great thanksgiving prayer in the Eucharist, as then, so still today. Many elements from liturgical thanksgivings and praise of the early Christian communities may have gone into the expressions of thanks at the beginnings of the Pauline letters. Paul writes his letters to the particular gatherings of the community that he imagines directly before him, but in them people spoke " full of the Spirit " to one another " in psalms and hymns and spiritual songs, singing and making melody to the Lord with all your heart, always and for everything giving thanks in the name of our Lord Jesus Christ to God the Father " (Eph. 5 : 19f.). " Though absent in body . . . , present in spirit " (cf. 1 Cor. 5 : 3), Paul joins, as he writes, in the thanks and praise of the assembled community. This gives his letters a liturgical form and makes them suitable for reading during divine worship.

³remembering before our God and Father your work of faith and labor of love and steadfastness of hope in our Lord Jesus Christ.

Paul is always giving thanks because his eyes see God at work everywhere. This thanksgiving of Paul rests on the foundation of a living remembrance. Because this is continual, his thanksgiving is also continual. How, then, do we learn continual thanksgiving? Obviously, by learning to remember, by learning to keep the mighty deeds of God always and everywhere present in the memory. Under the old covenant, solemn thanksgivings went up to God at the great feasts of Israel, when the past saving deeds of God were joyfully remembered. But now every moment is a great feast of remembrance, and our thanks must be continual because the saving deeds of God become present ever anew within the community of Christ; only we must see them and constantly have them before our eyes in faith. We can do this only if the Holy Spirit gives us the eyes for them, reminds us of them, and teaches us remembrance.

If God is at work in a community and Jesus Christ works in it through the Spirit, then we find in it faith, love, and hope. In this God manifests himself, for this cannot be achieved by Satan. But if faith, hope, and love are alive, they also become outwardly visible, and one recognizes faith by its effectiveness, love by the trouble it takes, and hope by its endurance. Christ can then say to such a community in praise: " I know your works, your toil, and your patient endurance " (Rev. 2:2).

The first thing we find is a powerful faith. The Apostle means the faith that he lists among the gifts of the Spirit, faith which makes the impossible possible, and can " remove mountains " (1 Cor. 13:2). He means talking and acting " in power, and in the Holy Spirit, and with full conviction " (1:5), which achieve visible works. In Christian communities there is an activity that is able to achieve what seems impossible, with great inner strength and spiritual enthusiasm. Further, there is in the community the painstakingness of love, the daily toils of the brethren, the selfless service. " By so toiling one must help the weak, remembering the words of the Lord Jesus . . . , ' it is more blessed to give than to receive ' " (Acts 20:35), so that no one in a community is hungry. More important still, however, the labor in " preaching and teaching " (1 Tim. 5:17), so that all attain salvation. Everything must be inspired by the will to serve and by love, from the work of charity to spiritual edification, from the service of administration to concern for the salvation of one's brother; the toil of love is involved in all the activities of the community, in all their breadth and depth.

Finally, there is also in a community the patient endurance in hope, full of confidence amid the many difficulties and persecutions that Christians have constantly to withstand. A living expectation of the coming Lord, however, endows one with patience and endurance. It was particularly strong in Thessa-

lonica. Where it exists, it is a great source of strength in the
life of the community.

Looking Back to the Beginnings
of the Community (1:4—2:16)

The Election and Call of the Thessalonians (1:4-10)

THE WORK OF THE MISSIONARIES (1:4-5)

*⁴For we know, brethren beloved by God, that he has chosen
you . . .*

Paul is talking to men who are loved by God. The Old Testament occasionally ventured this momentous statement about
great men of God such as Benjamin (Deut. 33:12), Moses (Sir.
45:1), and Solomon (Neh. 13:26). But Paul sees the great love
of God now directed also towards his Thessalonians. We look
at a man in another way if we know that God loves him; we
also behave differently towards him if we could only see our
neighbor in the light of the love of God, who has overwhelmed
him with graces or pursued him with love.

In both of the Epistles to the Thessalonians Paul uses
" brethren " as a form of address more than in any of the
other letters. This gives them their great warmth. Apart from
the " brotherhood " of the Old Testament people of God, in
which all call themselves " brothers " (cf. Acts 2:29, 37), the
communities of those who believed in Christ soon realized that
they were a " brotherhood " in a special way: " You have one

teacher, and you are all brethren " (Mt. 23:8). It was the risen Christ who first called his disciples this (Mt. 28:10; Jn. 20:17). Only if we see the Lord in our neighbor will we be able to recognize him as " loved by God," to address him as " brother," and be brotherly towards him. Brotherly love is always mediated by God; it comes from this knowledge.

How do we recognize God's love? Ultimately, in the fact that God has chosen us from eternity, for it is only in this way that the love of God is understood in its full depth. This " election " (Rom. 11:28) was once a privilege of Israel, but now it has also been imparted to the Thessalonians, who are gentiles. This became clear when Paul preached the gospel to them and they were converted. But does a serious conversion also mean that there has been an eternal election? Can every individual Christian who is a living member of a Christian community also consider himself as among the elect whose eternal blessedness is secured? It is true that there is no absolute certainty of salvation for the individual; yet the words of Paul encourage us to great confidence. For if God has called someone in time to a Christian community and given him the effective grace to live as a Christian, then that man can at least have the confident hope that he belongs to the elect of God. This confidence, however, is not based on one's own actions, but only on the Lord: " He who calls you is faithful, and he will do it " (5:24). At any rate, we too are addressed by Paul as " beloved by God." This knowledge of being chosen and loved by God can give one great happiness and drive away many temptations. A new life can begin from the moment at which someone confesses: God loves me.

⁵. . . *for our gospel came to you not only in word, but also in*

power and in the Holy Spirit and with full conviction. You know what kind of men we proved to be among you for your sake.

The three missionaries worked powerfully among the Thessalonians; they spoke in the power of the Spirit and with full conviction, not in empty words. Paul could also have written here (as in 1 Cor. 2:4): "My speech and my message were not in plausible words of wisdom, but in demonstration of the Spirit and power." In the words of preaching that is filled with the Spirit the Lord comes directly to the listener. His power is felt; his spirit is in the air. More than all the arguments, it is the living spiritual experience of the presence of the Lord that convinces, of him who works in the word of his missionaries and can be recognized behind it. Whoever wants to hear God's word must not seek worldly wisdom, and certainly not merely meaning and ideas: he must recognize the presence of the Spirit of Christ in it and want to find the presence of the Lord himself.

The three missionaries preached, filled with the Spirit and with great inner confidence. The power of Christ and the working of the Holy Spirit do not function separately from the preachers, or merely through them. It is precisely from personal conviction that the Spirit of the Lord speaks. It is the power of Christ that changes the hearts of the listeners. When the preacher speaks with his whole being, he is, in a special way, an instrument of the Lord who brings the Lord himself close to his listeners and makes them able to recognize him. This is the way that someone must preach and bear witness if living faith is to spring up.

Without service and devotion there is no spiritual work done anywhere, for the gifts of the Spirit only become active in self-sacrificing love. Everything happened for the sake of the Thessalonians, for their good. It was a " labor of love " (1 : 3) which performed a work of faith and founded the community in Thessalonica—a labor and toil that gave Paul no rest, night or day (cf. 2 : 9–12). The powers of the Spirit are always services, they are always given " for the good " of others (1 Cor. 12 : 7); they must serve to " build up " the community (1 Cor. 14 : 12). For it is only in devoted service, in personal commitment, that they become free and flowing, according to the measure of one's devotion.

THE ACCEPTANCE OF THE GOSPEL (1 :6–10)

⁶*And you become imitators of us and of the Lord, for you received the word in much affliction, [and yet] with joy inspired by the Holy Spirit; . . .*

We know what it means to follow Christ. But how could Paul expect that we imitate the Apostle too? Christ encounters us in the Apostle. Hence, to be a Christian means quite specifically to accept the apostolic way of life that comes from the Lord himself. But to take over the apostolic way of life means two things : the acceptance of faith and moral imitation. The Lord had given to his apostles the office of preaching, as well as the commission of being models of holiness. An apostle must not, therefore, keep both carefully separate. With him his office, which preaches and guarantees faith, and his life, which testifies to and demonstrates faith, form the greatest possible unity. Today, the bishops, as the successors of the apostles, can call for the acceptance of the teaching, but only saints, who are continuing into later times the exemplary perfection of the apostles, can call for moral imitation. Knowledge of faith and morals is attained by watching the apostles and then, further, those who live like them (Phil. 3:17). The Spirit of Christ is embodied in the church, in its saints, and in those who have office in it. What is asked of us is " church spirit " which submits to those in office and looks at the saints. This is how we follow Christ.

Wherever it is newly and freshly proclaimed, the word of God creates spiritual joy and inner happiness. In this joy we can see the working of the Holy Spirit, which evokes a happy assent to the truth of faith, a joyful acceptance. Preaching that does not arouse joy in the faithful obviously does not come sufficiently from the heart, and there is something the matter with a faith that does not make one happy.

This joy in faith continues even in affliction and persecution. Further down (2:14) we hear of this and in 2 Corinthians 8:2 Paul says of the communities of Macedonia: "In a severe test of affliction their abundance of joy . . . has overflowed." Naturally, sufferings bow one down, but the joy of faith comes from a deeper strength that grows, rather than declines, under persecution. All the joy of Easter is a fruit of the death of Jesus on the cross.

7. . . . so that you became an example to all the believers in Macedonia and in Achaia. 8aFor not only has the word of the Lord sounded forth from you in Macedonia and Achaia, . . .

The Christian community in the busy trading town of Thessalonica automatically became the " city set on a hill " (Mt. 5:14) for the whole of Greece, visible from afar off. If someone has adopted the word of God and the apostolic way of life, he himself has become a model from which others can see the right way of Christian living.

Christian life that is really alive propagates itself. A joyous faith cannot be hidden in one's heart; it rings out like a happy song that echoes over the mountains. Wherever the word of God is received with spiritual joy and has filled the heart, it naturally becomes a song that attracts others. A joyful faith affects other people; it is the mother of all apostolic work and all missionary success.

8b. . . *but [the news of] your faith in God has gone forth everywhere, so that we need not say anything [about it]. 9aFor they themselves report concerning us what a welcome we had among you,* . . .

The foundation of the first communities on European soil had caused great happiness everywhere in the young church. Christians have an eye for the workings of God, and they tell one another if they have seen God at work. The working of God is the only worthy subject of conversation. There is much " careless " talk (Mt. 12: 36). But it is important to relate with a joyful heart those events in which the working of God is revealed, for this kind of news arouses joy and confidence.

9b. . . *and how you turned to God from idols, to serve a living and true God,* . . .

In the synagogues all kinds of heathen gathered to sympathize with the Jewish faith. To them Paul had first to speak in the same way that Jewish preachers had done. These, too, had instructed the heathen on the existence of the one living true God, on the judgment of God that was to come, and then on the hoped-for Messiah. But these are not theoretical statements, but fundamental truths which give a new direction to life. If the living and true God is preached, then conversion of life is called for. This will result in a loving service of God and in confident hope. When a man realizes that God exists and who he is, his life is thrown off its course and set onto a new path.

Once one has been converted to God, this makes one's whole life a loving service of God. The knowledge of the one true God makes one the servant of God, and one's life becomes service. This knowledge does not reveal a new divinity who demands liturgical worship; rather, the living God wants to take one's whole life, with all its expressions, into his service. But this kind of service can no longer be restricted to religious worship; God wants not only the Sundays but the weekdays as well.

[10]. . . *and to wait for his Son from heaven, whom he raised from the dead, Jesus who delivers us from the wrath to come.*

Whoever has recognized the living God that demands our service also knows of the impending judgment. Therefore, there is as an adjunct to Christian conversion, a second basic attitude: the confident hope that knows it is free from the coming judgment. This trust can base itself only on Jesus. Part of the Christian message is the truth that God " will judge the world in righteousness " through Jesus, " whom he has appointed, and of this he has given assurance to all men by raising him from the dead " (Acts 17 : 31). In our text, however, Paul is not considering the just judgment that Christ will make according to one's works, but the coming punishment on the day of wrath. Jesus also will carry out this judgment of wrath; for then "the Lord Jesus is revealed from heaven with his mighty angels in flaming fire, inflicting vengeance upon those who do not know God and upon those who do not obey the gospel of our Lord Jesus" (2 Thess. 1:7f.). But to his own people he comes to "grant rest" (2 Thess. 1:7), as his very name says: as a saviour, "for he will save his people . . ." (Mt. 1:21). He will gather them about him and thus remove them in time from the judgment of wrath when it comes upon the world (4:17). "For God has not destined us for wrath, but to obtain salvation through our Lord Jesus Christ" (5:9). Thus the believer does not look forward to the coming of Christ full of slavish fear but with expectant confidence. Of course, the only man who can do that is one who does not look at his own failures, but sets all his hopes on the Lord, who wants to save him.

Paul had not only taught the Thessalonians to place all their hope on Christ; he had also urged them to wait for the return of Jesus, in a way that one longs for a visit from a dear friend. But one can only wait for somebody whose arrival one still hopes to experience, with whose possible coming one is at least reckoning. Our faith in no way gives us certain knowledge that we would definitely not experience the coming of the Lord. Rather, he tells us that the Lord will come "like a thief in the night" (5:2). Thus we are called to be always ready because the Lord can come at any time. Moreover, the coming of Jesus is a foregone reality for every single person at the moment of his death, the time of which he equally does not know. Thus to wait for Jesus is in any case bidden by wisdom, but beyond that it should be the living longing of one's life.

Looking Back Again to the Beginnings
of the Community (2:1–16)

Paul is led on by his thanksgiving and his memories, and comes
back to the heartwarming success that God has brought about in
Thessalonica. What was briefly mentioned in 1:4f. is now developed
in 2:1–12, and what was mentioned in 1:6–10 is taken up again in
2:13–16.

THE ENERGETIC AND SELFLESS WORK
OF THE MISSIONARIES (2:1–12)

²ʼ¹*For you yourselves know, brethren, that our visit to you was
not in vain;* ²*but though we had already suffered and been
shamefully treated [just before] at Philippi, as you know, we
had courage in our God to declare the gospel of God in the face
of great opposition.*

After the bad experiences in Philippi, it took a lot to start again
preaching the gospel in Thessalonica. In Philippi Paul and
Silvanus had been whipped, thrown into prison, and then forced
to leave the town. The Thessalonians would have been able to
see the scars on their bodies. But Paul, sensitive as he was, would
have felt their insulting treatment more deeply than their physical sufferings: " They have beaten us publicly, uncondemned,
men who are Roman citizens, and have thrown us into prison "
(Acts 16:37). In spite of all this Paul did not come spiritless and
empty to Thessalonica; on the contrary, he came " in power and
in the Holy Spirit and with full conviction " (1:5), so that the
first weeks had an immediate happy result.

Where did this inner fullness come from? From the quite personal relationship with God. Paul prayed. He tells us in 2 Corinthians 1:4 what can be experienced in prayer before God and from God: " [He] comforts us in all our affliction, so that we may be able to comfort those who are in any affliction, with the comfort with which we ourselves are comforted by God." From the close relationship with God in suffering comes the spontaneous desire and confidence to confess one's faith and preach it, as well as generosity and self-sacrifice, for which no exertion is too much (cf. 2:9–12).

³For our appeal does not spring from error or uncleanness, nor is it made with guile; . . .

It is not easy to give a message in God's name. Where is the proof that it is really proclaimed in God's name, that it comes from God? Paul stands quite unprotected with his statement that he has been " approved by God to be entrusted with the gospel " (2:4). He had frequently been asked for " proof ": Why should we believe that you speak in the name of God? Thus Paul is much occupied with the question of how his word can be made credible as what it is, as the word of God (cf. 2:13), of what is to be done in order that his preaching is not to be misunderstood and taken simply as a teaching based on human wisdom. But he does not adduce a lot of arguments to prove the divine origin of his gospel. As a pastor he knows what happens practically when men acquire faith: God's word must be experienced as such. But it is experienced in two ways: through the divine power that dwells within it (1:5), and the pureness of heart of its proclaimer (2:3). Paul is justified by the purity of his motives and the guilelessness of his method. His motives are selfless and pure, without any egoistic admixture. And the mode of his preaching is simple and straightforward, without any hidden *arrière-pensée*. But the more unselfish and self-sacrificial the preaching, the more convincing. Why? Because this selfless purity is ultimately not the work of man but of God. Where it exists, God is visibly at work; God becomes visible; God bears witness to himself. The unselfishness and purity of the homeless missionaries, the toiling pastors, the persecuted and despised witnesses: these are the quiet miracles by which God authenticates his gospel.

True, the listener must himself be pure and of good will in order to hear this quiet language of God. Not everyone understands it. But are not all the profound and sublime things of the world quiet and difficult to understand; do they not always require the involvement of one's whole heart? This is even more true of God's revealing word than of any philosophical truth and great work of art. It does not lie directly in one's path so that one stumbles over it. It is for those who are seeking pearls and are prepared to give anything for them (cf. Mt. 13:45f.). But these see God's authenticated signs as clear and powerful. And would it be worthy of God to be found in any other way?

⁴But just as we have been approved by God to be entrusted with the gospel, so we speak, not to please men, but to please God who tests our hearts.

The man whom God has entrusted with the preaching of the gospel has a high dignity, like a priest into whose hands God has entrusted the sacred. God must entrust a person with it. No one can arrogate this to himself. Preaching presupposes that one has been commissioned by God. In a truly divine trust God entrusts a man with the sacred in the confident assumption that he will pass it on properly. Thus God tests and weighs, seeking the person that is suitable for such a high office and commission, the person whom he is going to ask to perform it. There is something majestic about this trust. It makes us ashamed. It places a high obligation on us.

Paul preaches with the deepest sense of his responsibility before God, who will judge our hearts. He places his preaching within the framework of the inner responsibility of his conscience before God and is prepared to face the eternal judge with it. He knows that " if I were still pleasing men, I should not be a servant of Christ " (Gal. 1 : 10). Man can live only in terms of the Thou over against him. He cannot be autonomous. If he does not live theonomously, from God, he becomes heteronomous. If someone does not want to be dependent on God, he will be dependent on other things. To be dependent on God, however, is especially necessary for a missionary of God if he is to bring God's message and not simply preach himself.

5aFor we never used either words of flattery, as you know, . . .

Paul casts a side-glance at the many itinerant preachers of philosophy of the time, with which he on no account wants to be confused. Someone who is speaking the word of God cannot speak simply what men want to hear; he must speak the truth of God, " in season and out of season " (2 Tim. 4: 2). This is why the word of the Apostle is as incorruptible as the word of God. A preacher cannot leave out anything of what God has commissioned him to preach. Paul subtracts nothing in order to please men : to conform to some spirit of the age, the spirit of particular races or peoples, to please the rich or the poor, the educated or the uneducated. But this kind of incorruptibility makes the word he preaches credible.

[5b]. . . *or a cloak for greed, as God is witness;* [6a]*nor did we seek glory from other men, whether from you or from others,* . . .

Impure motives are generally hidden behind flattering talk. Paul rips the mask from the faces of the ingratiating speakers of his time to reveal their secret motives: it is only avarice that is behind all their talk. What won't someone preach in order to earn his money and be able to live well himself! Their ambition is even more dangerous: What isn't said and written in the world in order to acquire the esteem of men or to keep one's position! But Christians should be discerners of spirits, they should see through hidden intentions and recognize false motives. This safeguards against false teaching.

[6b]. . . *though we might have made demands as apostles of Christ.* [7]*But we were gentle among you, like a nurse taking care of her children.* [8]*So, being affectionately desirous of you, we were ready to share with you not only the gospel of God but also our own selves, because you had become very dear to us.*

Indeed, Paul, as an emissary of Christ, could appear with all honors, insist on his authority, and demand respect and reverence. But he prefers the way of gentle kindness and decides to serve unselfishly and self-sacrificially. In this he becomes like a mother—even more like a mother who is giving milk to her baby—still more like a mother who not only gives her child her milk, but pours herself out in all the love of her heart. Paul can be " in travail " for his pastoral children " until Christ be formed

in them " (cf. Gal. 4 : 19). This gentle, kind approach, this self-
sacrificial service, this generous love achieves great things. It
should stand behind all our words and works.

New converts need, " like newborn babes, . . . the pure
spiritual milk " (cf. 1 Pet. 2 : 2) Paul was able to give them. It
needs genuine devotion, a maternal approach, if someone wants
to give the word of God not only as hard bread, but also to the
small and weak as nourishing milk. Only great love is able to
do that. That is why the church's teaching office usually comes
to us in the form of the pastoral office; the teachers of the church
come as pastors. And everyone who wants to pass on the word
of God should try to do it in great love. Love will then tell him
what he has to say.

*For you remember our labor and toil, brethren; we worked
night and day, that we might not burden any of you, while we
preached to you the gospel of God. [10]You are witnesses, and God
also, how holy and righteous and blameless was our behavior to
you believers; . . .*

In his happy reminiscing about the foundation of the community, Paul has slipped back into the first weeks and months
of the community's life. It was a time of building-up in constant
individual pastoral work. However much Paul, as a conqueror
of the world, is concerned with founding and building communities, he does it only man by man. Pastoral love always
seeks the individual man.

Paul is not exaggerating when he also mentions his night
hours, for no doubt he was generally able to begin with his
pastoral work only in the evening, because during the day he
wanted to earn his bread by the work of his hands—perhaps in

Thessalonica as in Corinth as a tentmaker. " I coveted no one's silver or gold or apparel," he can say in Acts 20:33f.; " You yourselves know that these hands ministered to my necessities and to those who were with me." This kind of work to earn his living greatly increased the onerousness of the mission. But missionary activity, as he conceived it, required this. He had to be concerned that there should be no self-interest in preaching (cf. 2:3.5), so that his message should remain credible. This is why he did not let himself be supported by the Thessalonians. It is true that this would have saved him a lot of time and labor that he could have devoted to his essential pastoral activity; but Paul, though concerned to press forward, is surprisingly untroubled about this problem of time, but on the other hand very concerned that his preaching should come out the right way. Less pastoral work, but performed selflessly and in apostolic poverty, produces more fruit than constant pastoral work that cannot present its word in such a way that it lights up purely as God's word. The light of preaching has always had particular brilliance when it shone forth from the lampstand of apostolic poverty. Selflessness lets the light of God blaze out.

[11]. . . *for you know how, like a father with his children, we exhorted each one of you and encouraged you and charged you* [12]*to lead a life worthy of God, who calls you to his own kingdom and glory.*

Paul sees himself not only as a mother (2:7f.) in his role of pastor but also as a father in his role of teacher. For with the Thessalonians, as with the Corinthians (cf. 1 Cor. 4:15f.), he " became your father in Christ Jesus through the gospel." But a father has the right of correction, and because he is impelled by fatherly love, Paul has no fear of being importunate. After all, love can be allowed a lot. It is only in such a visible love that a person is able to correct, encourage, and urge.

The Apostle does not justify his exhortation now in the same way as he had to in his preaching to win converts: he does not tell them to think of how they would stand before the judgment of God and to seize the saving hand of Christ (cf. 1:9f.). After conversion and baptism the main thing is for us to respond to God, who calls each one of us in a quite personal way, who has already called us in Christ, who will call us into the glory of his kingdom, and who is calling us now, urgently, in this very moment, the time for decision, the eleventh hour. Whether our thoughts rove into the past or into the future, or whether they want to rest in the present, we always discover ourselves as men called and summoned, we always encounter God calling us. Thus it is very important that I recognize that God is calling me now, at this very moment, insistently.

Show yourselves worthy of the call of God; think of what you owe him, Paul exhorts us. God's call is certainly a great grace. This reference to God's grace seems more effective to Paul than the reminder of the coming judgment, for grace puts an obligation on us. The grateful return of love should be the basic melody of our life. The God who calls us wants a grateful and loving response.

God calls us to his royal kingdom, to his own blessed world. This is the epitomy of all happiness. What awaits us in God's world is expressed by a single phrase: we will be surrounded, transformed, and enraptured by the luminous glory of God. To have such a goal before one changes one's life. Much that previously seemed worth striving for and indispensable now loses its value. With such a goal before him man can also put up with much affliction and injustice.

THE ACCEPTANCE OF THE GOSPEL (2:13–16)

Again, as in 1:6–10, Paul's mind moves on from his own missionary activity to the joyful event that the Thessalonians have been converted and accepted the faith.

[13]And we also thank God constantly for this, that when you received the word of God which you heard from us, you accepted it not as the word of man but as what it really is, the word of God, which is at work in you believers.

It is not only the believers whom God has summoned that have to be grateful, but also the missionaries, from their very office. After all, God has done a great thing through them. This thanks of Paul is never ending. A constant prayer of thanks is not possible for man by himself; but it is the spirit of Christ that constantly renders thanks in Paul and makes thanksgiving a basic attitude in him. Since the days of the Apostle this apostolic thanksgiving has continued: it continues to sound forth in the church's celebration of the Eucharist and in the divine office. The church constantly gives thanks for the grace that God has given to us. What God has done to us is so great that it must give rise to world-wide and incessant rejoicing.

The Thessalonians have recognized that his word is the word of God, "the word of God which you heard from us," " the message that we brought you as God's message," as Paul somewhat clumsily says. He would never have been satisfied if the Thessalonians had merely regarded his teaching as sensible, clear, and acceptable. The human word also can be sensible and clear; but God's word differs from all philosophies or ideologies by virtue of the fact that it is a message from God. The important thing is that the word of the preaching is accepted as the word of God, the word of revelation. Whoever listens to a sermon must hear in it that God himself is speaking to him. If he hasn't heard that then he has understood nothing.

Paul presents God's word as an independent person: it achieves its own work independently of him, even long after the preacher has left. The difference between God's word and the human word is that it has its own effective power and is successful. " For the word of God is living and active, sharper than any two-edged sword " (Heb. 4:12).

14For you, brethren, became imitators of the churches of God in Christ Jesus which are in Judea; for you suffered the same things from your own countrymen as they did from the Jews, . . .

The word of God shows its power especially in the fact that it makes one capable of suffering, of confessing it, and even suffering martyrdom for it. A human word cannot achieve this. The word of God has an inner orientation towards the cross.

The fate of Christ became the fate of the church. The Thessalonians have received a share in the general fate of the church. The sufferings that the Jewish-Christian communities had to undergo from the beginning now come to the first foundations of gentile Christians. It becomes clear everywhere that the church is a church of martyrs. That the word of God was successful in Thessalonica and that the true " church " was founded is shown precisely in the fact that the community had from the beginning one characteristic of all Christian communities: that of being persecuted. The knowledge of being exposed to persecutions has been with the church from the beginning and makes it ready for them and steadfast.

According to ancient prophecy (Mic. 7:6), it is characteristic of the last time that enmity for the sake of God springs up in one's own people, even within one's own family. The Christian can become very lonely for the sake of God, and find himself in deep and painful opposition even to those who are dear to him.

[15]... *who killed both the Lord Jesus and [before him] the prophets, and drove us out, and displease God and oppose all men* [16a]*by hindering us from speaking to the gentiles that they may be saved . . .*

Paul is possibly thinking of the fact that the gentile persecutions in Thessalonica went back to Jewish intrigues, which also pursued him in Berea and nowhere gave him rest. The Jews persecuted those who believed in Christ in the belief that they were thereby " offering service to God " (Jn. 16:2). Persecutions from religious motives are always particularly dangerous; they have a virulence that can only come from a false religion of revelation.

The measure was not yet full with the crucifixion of Christ, for it was God's saving will—as Paul knew in a more living way than anyone before him—to save the gentiles also before it is too late, to bring the gospel to all heathen people before the end; only then can the end come (cf. Mk. 13:10). Because God wants the salvation of the heathen, he wants missionary activity. Anyone who knows about the saving will of God cannot ignore the idea of missionary work.

Even the ancient pagans saw that the Jews, with their faith in the one God, were different from them. This, combined with other reasons, led even in the ancient world to alienation and antisemitism. Paul seems to take up the unjust accusation that the Jews were the enemies of all men; but he understands it in a different, quite new way. He himself wishes to be banished, separated from Christ, in place of his " brethren," " kinsmen by race " (Rom. 9:3), so much does he love them. But in the present case they give a certain justification to the ugly reproach when they put obstacles in the way of Paul's mission to the gentiles. They are hindering the work of God's mercy, which desires the salvation of all men, including that of the gentiles.

16b*so [now] as always to fill up the measure of their sin. But God's wrath has now come upon them at last!*

One might imagine that the measure of the sins of the murderers of the prophets (Mt. 23:32) would have been full when they finally also murdered the " Son." This was the cry of the first martyr, Stephen (Acts 7:52): " Which of the prophets did not your fathers persecute? And they killed those who announced beforehand the coming of the Righteous One, whom you have now betrayed and murdered." But after the crucifixion of Jesus, God in his infinite mercy had allowed Israel an interval for a change of heart (Acts 2:38ff.). " God, desiring to show his wrath and to make known his power, has endured with much patience the vessels of wrath made for destruction " (Rom. 9:22). Only when Israel will also " kill and persecute " the Lord's " prophets and apostles " (Lk. 11:49ff.) will the measure of their sins be full and vengeance taken for all the blood they have spilt. This final act of the tragedy is what Paul is now constantly experiencing personally: the final hardening of the heart of Israel.

Paul could see many signs that the threats Jesus made of punishment to Israel would now soon be fulfilled; but this was especially true when he experienced this hardening of heart by the people, the persecution of those who brought the faith, and the hindering of missionary work. But at the time he wrote the sentence, he was working in Corinth as a tentmaker in the house of the couple Aquila and Priscilla, who had shortly before been expelled with other Jews from Rome under the emperor Claudius. Perhaps Paul saw the beginning of the end in a concrete way in this event: the expulsion of the Jews from the capital by the Roman ruler of the world appeared to him perhaps as the beginning of the disaster which was to come in A.D. 70, when the Roman armies destroyed Jerusalem and the temple. This contemporary event, which deeply affected the Apostle, may be the reason for the particular severity of his language here. He knows that later, despite the imminent judgment, God will keep ready salvation for Israel and has not finally withdrawn his mercy.

Information: The Concern of the Apostle for the Constancy of the Community (2:17—3:11)

Now at last, after lengthy reminiscing and expressions of gratitude, Paul comes to the main part of his communication. He speaks of the period since his separation from the community, his longing for them, and his loving care for them, though he is far off. Paul had been seriously concerned about whether the newly founded community had stood up to its various afflictions. But now Timothy had brought good news, and so Paul reverts again to the thanksgiving and the intercessory prayer with which he had started (3:7–11.12f.). For just as Paul had first to render thanks (1:2—2:16) for the beginnings of the community through God's grace, so now he must also be grateful that God had given the community such steadfastness (2:17—3:11). When Paul thinks of the community in which God has done such joyous work, then he must constantly give thanks. All his words come from the profoundest depth of his being, where he dwells continually in the presence of God and whence continual prayer comes.

Paul's Longing for the Community and Timothy's Mission (2:17—3:11)

PAUL LONGING (2:17–20)

[17]*But since we are bereft of you, brethren, for a short time, in person not in heart, we endeavored the more eagerly and with great desire to see you face to face;* [18a]*because we wanted to come [back] to you—I, Paul, again and again—, . . .*

When he was driven out, Paul had to leave the young community in an unsettled state and in need of help. But it is not only his apostolic conscience that urges him back to it, but also love and affection. Paul has been torn from his children like a father (2:11), like a mother (2:7f.), and now he longs for the community in great affection and love. His pastoral love arouses in him paternal, maternal, and fraternal feelings; his whole human heart is moved by them. It is the whole man who is the pastor here.

[18b]*. . . but Satan hindered us.*

It does not seem at all important to Paul to name the earthly obstacles that have prevented his return to Thessalonica; he knows who has really prevented him. Like a flash of lightning, this hard sentence, coming in the midst of words of love, lights up the seriousness of the situation. For a brief moment we can cast a glance at the field of action on which missionary and pastoral work take place; it is a battlefield on which the contest is raging between God and Satan. The more someone comes from God in his pastoral work, the more he will come up against the antagonist of God in his work and recognize him as his real enemy. It is necessary to see the reality: in and behind all earthly events there is a war being waged between God and his enemy.

¹⁹*For what is our hope or joy or crown of boasting before our Lord Jesus at his coming? Is it not you [among others]?* ²⁰*For you [also] are our glory and joy.*

Paul longs for the glorious coming of the Lord (cf. 1:10), when there will be great rejoicing (4:13–18). Paul does not yet call the birth of Christ an " arrival," the " parousia," and his eschatological coming is not yet for him his " return." For only the parousia realizes the full salvation that the prophets have promised. Only then is the fullness of grace poured out. Whoever longs so deeply for full salvation looks forward to the coming of Christ, not only backwards to his birth. It is true that " the grace of God has appeared for the salvation of all men " (Tit. 2:11f.). But it is also true that the first coming of Jesus is only a pledge of what he will give us at the end. Hence our longing should be for the future.

On the Damascus road Paul had received quite personally the commission to preach the gospel of Christ among the pagans, to call the pagans to Christ. Paul looks forward to declaring his commission accomplished and to presenting to the Lord the communities he has won when he comes in his royal glory, so that he " may be proud in the day of Christ " (Phil. 2:16). His own hope of being saved depends on his having been able to carry out his commission successfully. That great day will bring him joy and honor. But this joy and this honor are already dilating his soul, since he is almost beside himself with gratitude " for all the joy which we feel for your sake before our God " (3:9). This is the hope that someone may have who knows that " by the grace of God I am what I am, and his grace towards me was not in vain " (1 Cor. 15:10). This results in joy and pride. It is nothing but ingratitude if a person looks only at his sins, but not at the great things that God's grace has done in him and through him. This " short-sightedness " which comes from a sad love of self-abasement, vitiates a Christian's life. For a self-abasement which does not think it dare see and acknowledge the miracles of God's grace in one's own life comes in fact from the devil.

Timothy's Mission (3:1-5)

³:¹*Therefore, when we could bear it no longer, we were willing to be left behind at Athens alone, ²ᵃand we sent Timothy, our brother, and God's servant in the gospel of Christ, . . .*

Paul had just asked Silvanus and Timothy to leave Berea and come to him in Athens (Acts 17:15); but the news of the dangerous oppressions in Thessalonica (2:14; 3:3f.) made another parting necessary. This gnaws at his heart. The decision to remain alone in Athens is not an easy one for him. Timothy is like a brother to him, he calls him his " beloved child." There is a warm relationship between him and his " helper " (cf. Acts 19:22), in which he makes nothing of his superior position. He knows himself united with his helpers like a brother and a father.

Paul calls his " brother " Timothy here " God's servant." Thus he detaches his helper from himself (cf. Rom. 16:21) and places him in the closest possible immediacy to God. Paul knows that they are God's helpers. He knows that he has been entrusted with the proclamation of the gospel by God and is responsible to him alone (2:4). Someone who knows that God has taken him into his service in this way cannot regard his helpers in the same work as subservient to him; as laborers on the same work of God they are both on the same level, despite any official subordination. Whoever sees his own helpers as " God's servants " makes them his " brothers." The relationship between men is ordered in terms of God: whoever thinks in terms of God sees everything in the right way.

²ᵇ. . . *to establish you in your faith and to exhort you,* ³ᵃ*that no one be moved by these afflictions.*

In his concern Paul has profound knowledge of the dangers in the persecuted young community. What help is there? If faith is in danger, there is the strengthening and exhorting brotherly word. Paul sets his hope on this. The strengthening of the brethren comes about through a " grace " which comes from the Lord himself and gives their hearts " eternal comfort and good hope " (2 Thess. 2:16f.), it comes through our " spiritual gift " (Rom. 1:11). It is God (Rom. 16:25), Christ (2 Thess. 2:3) who must " strengthen." For the capacity to give strength and comfort is a charism (Rom. 12:8). God must " make his appeal " through men (2 Cor. 5:20). Thus gifts of the Spirit are necessary if Christians who are threatened by persecution and temptation are to be preserved in their faith. In this situation all the help comes from a brotherly word in which the Spirit of God is at work.

³ᵇ*You yourselves know that this is to be our lot. ⁴For when we were with you, we told you beforehand that we were to suffer affliction; just as it has come to pass, and as you [now] know.*

We constantly find something like the phrase: " But you already know this." Paul knows that he can only teach successfully where someone else has already taught before. If God's grace does not give one inner understanding, then even an apostle teaches in vain. The " inner teacher " speaks in our heart and makes it possible for the word of the human teacher to be believed and its truth to be experienced in one's own life. But this became a reality in a new covenant: God teaches everyone directly in his heart through the Holy Spirit. Without any inner spiritual experience of the words of the apostles, no sermon, particularly one on the necessity of suffering, will achieve anything. It will be a good thing to listen a lot to the inner teacher and to grow in the understanding and knowledge that comes from him.

Paul does not tell us why Christians must be persecuted; rather, he simply says that God has ordained it. If someone has understood that God wants it like that, that it must be like that according to his decree, then that must suffice for him. He needs no further explanations. Whoever has seen God's will in it has understood enough and can accept it.

But perhaps Paul had explained this divine decree to the Thessalonians in his oral instruction by saying something like: " Do not be surprised at the fiery ordeal which comes upon you to prove you, as though something strange were happening to you . . . For the time has come for judgment to begin with the household of God . . ." (1 Pet. 4:12, 17. Christians must suffer because they are living in the last times, in the time of the great tribulation (cf. Mk. 13:9–24). This is part of the fate of the church (cf. 2:14), to be there for affliction in this last time of tribulation. Such a statement leads into boundless depths. Who can plumb them?

Paul could come to Thessalonica at that time as a prophet and prophesy coming persecutions. Not that he had received special revelations about them, but he had understood the prophecies of the Lord and the decree of God about the church in the last times. But God's prophetic word is " a lamp shining in a dark place, until the day dawns and the morning star rises . . ." (2 Pet. 1:19). In this light the believer sees reality soberly and clearly even in dark times. It gives a realistic understanding of time and makes it possible to act with assuredness historically in the world, both in private and in public life. The Christian does not live on allusions, he does not indulge in daydreams, but, rather, is ready for everything and always well prepared.

⁵For this reason, when I could bear it no longer, I sent that I might know [how it was with] your faith, for fear that somehow the tempter had tempted you and that our labor would [thus] be in vain.

Behind the persecutions of the Christians stands their real originator, the tempter, Satan himself. Paul sees that his power is great (cf. 2:18), so that his caring love allows him no peace. He knows that the time of the great rebellion is near (cf. 2 Thess. 2:3). In the temptations of the last times Christian faith can be so imperiled that an anxious pastor like Paul must worry about souls. Whoever is seriously led into such " temptation " already seems lost. That is why the believer must daily pray to " be delivered from wicked and evil men " (cf. 2 Thess. 3:2), " de-

liver us from evil " (2 Thess. 3:3), " lead us not into temptation . . ."

Paul's Joy at Timothy's Report (3 :6–11)

TIMOTHY'S REPORT (3:6)

*⁶But now that Timothy has come to us from you, and has
brought us the good news of your faith and love, and reported
that you always remember us kindly and long to see us, as we
long to see you, . . .*

Paul attaches great importance to the news that the community is
still thinking of him. In this he sees more than personal attach-
ment. It is not enough for a community to have a powerful
faith and active brotherly love (cf. 1:3). A community does not
" stand fast in the Lord " (3:8) if it is isolated; the Lord is fully
present only in the unity of the church. This unity is shown in
connection with the apostolic office. From the earliest times this
is expressed particularly in the form of the memory in the
liturgy. But here more is meant: a memory which embraces
one's whole life. If Christians remember one another in love
before God this creates a powerful inner unity. In this way the
church is brought into being, because the Lord is present in this
unity. All the gaps are closed through which the powers of the
underworld and of evil could penetrate into the life of Christians.
    These Christians went to some pains to preserve unity: a two-
way journey of 500 miles was at that time full of difficulties. The
Apostle and the community longed for a reunion; they were concerned to make a personal contact. There is no church unity

without the apostolic office that must demand obedience and without subordination to the officials whom God has set in their place. But all the legal relationships are enmeshed here in personal relations of warm love. The high, primary church office, that of the Apostle, conceals its authority and claims in overwhelming love. Warmth of heart characterizes the style of the apostolic office. And the whole life of the apostolic communities was warm and loving. Affection was the *lingua franca* of these Christians; it made many things clear.

Paul's Joy and His Wish (3:7–11)

⁷. . . for this reason, brethren, in all our distress and affliction we have been comforted about you through your faith; ⁸for now we [are able to] live if [we know that] you stand fast in the Lord.

Pastoral care for Paul was real care. To live with the worry whether the young community had withstood the persecution was no life for Paul. And it was like being saved from death, a great " comfort," when he then received good news. The question of the salvation of one's brother can be experienced with such a depth that it is a matter of life or death. From this care comes pastoral care.

It is not self-pity when Paul speaks here and elsewhere in strong language of his afflictions. We do not understand Paul's sufferings if we only see them from outside. Paul has been sent and lives for love; his is an exposed, unprotected, and lonely life, and he lives it in unusual intellectual and spiritual clarity and consciousness. Thus his sufferings become from within " Christ's sufferings " (2 Cor. 1:5).

⁹For what thanksgiving can we render to God for you, for all the joy which we feel for your sake before our God . . .

Paul notes that the constant thanksgiving (2:13; cf. 1:2), which does not let him get beyond the opening of the letter, is still completely inadequate. In thanksgiving man cannot do everything that he ought. All the benefits of God call for conversion into gratitude and should be carried back to God in the form of thanksgiving; but there is no end to this.

If a man lives before the countenance of God, his inner being expands and, as if clairvoyant, he experiences the working of God. At the same time great spiritual depths become alive in him and thus the " joy in the Holy Spirit " (Rom. 14:17). It is the joy that is the fruit of the Spirit (Gal. 5:22). The man who lives before God sees things new; he experiences deeply and knows what joy is.

¹⁰. . . praying earnestly night and day that we may see you face to face and supply what is lacking in your faith?

Paul does not say much about the obvious weaknesses (3:5) and shortcomings in a community, because his gaze is wholly directed towards what God is achieving. But he is still very concerned and ponders what help he can give where he sees shortcomings. It is the inadequacies of one's fellow men which show whether one is truly living for God. They are a touchstone as to whether he is able to accept such shortcomings in silence but at the same time with loving care.

¹¹Now may our God and Father himself, and our Lord Jesus, direct our way to you, . . .

Paul knows that pastoral work and the apostolate is the achievement of God, but the real enemy is Satan. If it is Satan who blocks the way (2:18), only God can remove the obstacles. That is why prayer alone can help to clear the path. Only he can use the right means who adequately assesses the obstacles in faith. Where Satan is the opponent, it will be necessary to use prayer.

A Final Blessing (3:12–13)

[12]. . . *and may the Lord make you increase and [even] abound in love to one another and to all men, as we do to you, . . .*

If the faith of the Thessalonians still shows shortcomings (3:10), then they are in love, which can never reach its full measure. For the measure of love is only full when it overflows. Love cannot be measured, for it has its measure only in its overflowing measurelessness.

Love has a shape and a structure: it is primarily always " love of the brethren " (cf. 4:9); this makes a community into a brotherhood (1 Pet. 3:8; 5:9). Brotherly love is mutual love in giving and taking; it creates community and unity. When the measure of brotherly love is full, when a community is a brotherhood of mutual love, then the measure flows over, and love for everyone is born. Thus in " love of the brethren " we find the spring of brotherly affection for everyone " (2 Pet. 1:7), which can even finally become the love of one's enemy, because it can also love where it finds no answering love. He who " loves the brotherhood " will also " honor all men " (1 Pet. 2:17) and be concerned not only for the well-being of his brother in faith, but also of every neighbor (cf. 5:15). But the school of this love is

Christian "brotherhood," in which first brotherly love and then the love for all is learned. Whoever has learnt brotherly love in this school has thus also become capable of love of his neighbors. If the talk is of brotherly love, then Paul wants to be part of it: this is what should unite even the highest office-holder—and the apostle is the highest office-holder in the church—with the faithful. Love is the principle of all church government and all pastoral care. All the work of a pastor is service and the expression of love.

[13]... *so that he may establish your hearts unblamable in holiness before our God and Father, at the coming of our Lord Jesus with all his saints.*

At his great parousia the Lord will gather and save his people when God's wrathful judgment will burst upon the world (cf. 1:10). The holy angels accompanying him (2 Thess. 1:7) will then be sent out to "gather his elect" (Mk. 13:27). But will Christ also be able to help when we then stand naked and unprotected before the judgment seat of God? The Lord makes us capable of this also, now and always (cf. also 5:23f.), by giving love to our hearts (3:12) and thus strengthening us. All growth in goodness comes from the Lord and thus must be asked of him.

INSTRUCTION IN THE CHRISTIAN LIFE
(4:1—5:24)

The introductory thanksgiving (1:2—3:13) had provided a framework for the whole first part of the letter. Similarly, the final exhortation is also expanded to make a second part (4:1—5:24). But we should not understand the second part of the letter as a moral sermon, for more is involved than that. Paul not only exhorts, but also gives apostolic instruction, fundamental guidelines for Christian life in a community and beyond it. In a very simple and brotherly form he presents here five points of the Christian way of life.

This Christian tradition (2 Thess. 2:5) goes back to Christ himself (1:6), but the Apostle presents it in the name of Christ. True, it is adapted in the Holy Spirit to the particular situation of the community in Thessalonica, but it still remains universally valid and binding for the communities and Christians of all times. The Apostle tries here to give a fundamental formulation of what is pleasing to God (4:1), what his " will " is (4:3; 5:18), as he emphasizes in the introduction and the conclusion. These directions give the basis in the church for the shaping of all Christian life. Hence it is absolutely essential to place oneself firmly on this apostolic foundation and no other.

The Life That Is Pleasing to God (4:1–3a)

4:1Finally, brethren, we beseech and exhort you in the Lord Jesus, that as you learnt from us how you ought to live and [thus] to please God just as you are [now] doing, you do so

47

more and more. *²For you know what instructions we gave you through the Lord Jesus.*

When an apostle exhorts, he has the Lord behind him; it is the latter who exhorts through him. The Apostle teaches as one who " has the Spirit of God " (1 Cor. 7:40). Thus we can " know and [be persuaded] in the Lord Jesus " of the will of God (Rom. 14:14) and hope for many things (Phil. 2:19). His ordinances become those of divine justice and spiritual instructions " in the name of the Lord Jesus Christ " (2 Thess. 3:6; 1 Cor. 1:10), which are binding in conscience and demand obedience. It is not just anyone who is exhorting us here.

These sort of apostolic instructions have become traditions in the church. How can we know what is good and right? We examine what was always considered good and proper within the church. It is in the life and consciousness of faith of the church, that is in church tradition, that the Holy Spirit has interpreted and presented the will of God; whoever follows these traditions is obedient to the Lord himself who makes us know his holy will in this way.

The viewpoint from which Paul sees all moral action is important: it is done to please God. Orientation towards the judgment to come (4:6; cf. 1:13) was one of the fundamental elements of the proclamation (cf. 1:10). The chief thing is to please him who will " test our hearts " (2:4). All moral action is to be religious obedience. In everything that he does the Christian seeks in love the faith of God. It is true that only he will achieve this kind of religious obedience who lives towards the future in as real a way as Paul and who knows that God will come as a judge. Only if someone looks constantly towards the end will he be constant and faithful in obedience.

Paul corrects himself: the Thessalonians do not need to be exhorted any more to adopt a way of life that is pleasing to God. It is enough to exhort them to continue to progress in this way. There is no limit to the endeavor to please God. That is why those who are already converted and have made up their minds to live a life pleasing to God must be constantly reminded to please him. In this we can only increase without ever coming to an end. For if God is the Lord, when has the servant of such a Lord ever been completely obedient?

3a*For this is the will of God, your sanctification:* . . .

Here, in an introductory way, and again at the end (5:23), Paul points out that the purpose of all moral action is sanctification, which God already demanded in the Old Testament: " Consecrate yourselves, therefore, and be holy, for I am holy . . . For I am the Lord who brought you up out of the land of Egypt, to be your God; you shall therefore be holy, for I am holy " (Lev. 11:44f.). There has probably never been a better formulation of what God wants of us. But in the New Testament sanctification no longer consists in sacrifice and the observance of ritual practices, as the pagan might think; nor does it consist of the fulfillment of laws and adherence to traditions, as the Jews considered, but rather what is demanded is moral sanctification. This sanctification comes from God (5:23), from Christ (3:13; cf. also 1 Cor. 1:30); it is his work (3:12f.); it is the work of the Holy Spirit (cf. 4:8; 2 Thess. 2:13; 1 Pet. 1:2), and thus it becomes our own task to which we are called (4:7). Now our life has a valid goal, beside which every other one is unimportant, even wrong. But we must listen carefully: God's will, the goal of our lives that he has set for us, is not self-perfection, self-realization, but sanctification: we must seek to please God (4:1) and obediently do his will.

A Warning Against Pagan Vices (4:3b–8)

Paul first gives a number of warnings. After all, he is writing to former pagans who have turned away from " idols, to serve a living and true God " (1:9). But although they have become Christians, they remain in the old pagan environment. Thus even after their baptism they first had to be warned to persevere in their new " service of God " and not to fall back into the two vices that were characteristic of pagan life at that time: sexual license and avarice. Again and again Paul has to exhort and warn new converts in these or similar terms: " But immorality and all impurity or covetousness must not even be named among you, as is fitting among saints . . . but instead let there be thanksgiving. Be sure of this, that no immoral or impure man, or one who is covetous (that is an idolater), has any inheritance in the kingdom of Christ and of God."

A Warning Against Sexual License (4:3b–5)

³ᵇ*. . . that you abstain from immorality; ⁴that each one of you know how to take a wife for himself in holiness and honor, ⁵[but that means] not in the passion of lust like heathen who do not know God; . . .*

Pagans at that time did not consider it wrong to indulge themselves sexually as much as they liked. If a new convert lost his relationship with God and no longer conceived his life as the service of God, this was often soon seen in sexual license; he risked falling back into pre-Christian habits. If he no longer loves God, then there is a vacuum in his senses and his longings; his heart is darkened; he no longer sees any light; the concupiscence of the human heart overpowers him.

Paul knows what advice he must give to the former pagans, in whose environment the ideal of marriage with one person and for a lifetime scarcely existed: " But because of the temptation to immorality, each man should have his own wife " (1 Cor. 7 : 2). Thus he first urges his converts to conclude a proper legal marriage, but also to conduct themselves in marriage in the right way. The marriage is to be holy and honored, it is not to be a matter of lustful passion, which dishonors both one's own body and that of one's partner (cf. 1 Cor. 6: 18). The sexual drive can easily enslave and devalue one's partner. But where one is striving for a " sanctification " and seeks " to please God " (4: 1–3), his marriage also will partake of holiness and honor. Faith in God builds a house in which one can live worthily even as a man. Living faith transforms and penetrates all the circumstances of one's life.

A Warning Against Dishonesty in Business (4 :6–8)

6a. . . that no man transgress, and wrong his brother [in business], . . .

Business ambition, which seeks to outwit the other, was a special characteristic of pagan life in the large trading town of Thessalonica. With adultery this egoistic desire for gain was the chief characteristic of the life of the time. But this desire for gain remained a danger for the human heart for as long as man remains an egoistic individualist. But if he sees his brother in his business associates, the relationship with his neighbor is changed, business morality included. The word "brother" contains a great and miraculous power. In brotherly love many problems are solved.

6b. . . because the Lord is an avenger in all these things, as we solemnly forewarned you. 7For God has not called us for uncleanness, but in holiness.

The idea of the judgment of God belongs not only to the first sermon, which called the listeners to faith and conversion (1:10); it stands over the whole of Christian life (2:4; 3:13). For those who are called by God it even acquires a quite new urgency. In our baptism God gave us the Holy Spirit, who sanctifies us. But he works our sanctification in order that we may be saved (2 Thess. 2:13; cf. 1 Thess. 5:23f.). If anyone acts contrary to him, then he will all the more deserve to face judgment. Christians also must work out their salvation "with fear and trembling" (Phil. 2:12).

8Therefore, whoever disregards this [that we have said], disregards not man but God, who gives his Holy Spirit to you.

The instruction that Paul gives here has the full weight of an apostolic instruction. It is fundamental to Christian life and is to pass into the tradition of the church. Behind it stands God with his authority and the Holy Spirit. Paul speaks sternly and energetically because he sees the approaching danger. He not only sees that the newly converted Christians are in moral peril in their immoral environment; there is also the danger that all their principles become softened and that the moral tradition that always existed in the church is pushed aside as no longer binding.

Christians are to find their moral principles in the teaching of the church and not be guided by the views of their pre-Christian period.

An Exhortation to Brotherly Love and an Industrious Life (4:9–12)

Now Paul gives a number of exhortations: he gives us a brief but comprehensive picture which should guide the whole of Christian life in community and public relationships: the life of the community should be governed by brotherly love and social life by decency.

Brotherly Love Within the Community and Towards Other Christians (4:9–10)

⁹*But concerning love of the brethren you have no need to have anyone write to you, for you yourselves have been taught by God to love one another;* ¹⁰*and indeed you do love all the brethren throughout Macedonia. But we exhort you, brethren, to do so more and more.*

Now the time has come when no one has to instruct another, because all know God, " from the least of them to the greatest " (Jer. 31:34). Now God himself is the teacher of all (Mt. 23:8), and all are taught by God. It is not by chance that God has first " taught " the Thessalonians about brotherly love. God teaches within men, by pouring love into their hearts. But love desires to love. Where God instructs men in this way in love and through love and himself becomes their teacher, they will automatically become " brothers " to one another: " You have one teacher and you are all brethren " (Mt. 23:8). At a time when the eschatological teaching of God has begun, there is a new brotherhood of those converted by God, in which brotherly love reigns. This is what gives their hearts steadfastness and makes them blameless and holy for the coming judgment (3:12f.).

Brotherly love in the community has proved itself in the fact that someone who came to the large trading town from Macedonia was received hospitably as a brother. Good relations were kept up with the brethren who had to live scattered in the country. It can be seen how the church grows out of love for the brethren: it impels towards solidarity, communion, unity; it lets no one be lonely.

An Honorable Public Life (4:11–12)

[11a]. . . aspire to live quietly, mind your own affairs, . . .

There are things wrong in the community. Some members seem to enjoy standing around the marketplace getting involved in discussions on all public affairs, while at the same time neglecting their work. Paul is not defending a *petit bourgeois* ideal of having no responsibility for public affairs. Rather, the background here is the living expectation of the Lord. In the expectation of the coming of Christ many unimportant things lose their false importance; it is no longer necessary to say much about them. All restless business is unmasked while the everyday things that relate to the duties of one's own station become very important. In the light of the return of Christ one sees the things of life soberly and learns to distinguish between what is important and what is not. One also learns to accommodate oneself to the circumstances in which one is placed. Even a narrow and small sphere of life now becomes a serious concern. We are to apply all our ability to filling it properly.

[11b]. . . *and to work with your hands, as we charged you;* [12]*so that you may command the respect of outsiders, and be dependent on nobody.*

Many were probably lonely and in need of work. Perhaps the charitable work of the community, which supported those in need, had also become a temptation for some Christians. Every Christian, however, should apply his ability to not being dependent on support from his brethren, as did Paul (2:9; 2 Thess. 3:8) in order to give the Thessalonians " an example " (2 Thess. 3:9). " It is more blessed to give than to receive " (Acts 20:35). Love does not want to be a burden on anyone; it does not like being waited on.

The early Christians had " favor with all the people " (Acts 2:47), and Paul exhorts: " Give no offense to Jews or to Greeks or to the church of God, just as I try to please all men in everything I do, not seeking my own advantage, but that of many, that they may be saved " (1 Cor. 10:32). Christian life should shine out. Even unbelievers, before whom one cannot speak of " sanctification " and " the will of God " (cf. 4:3), are to see that their own ideal of human " decency " finds its fulfillment in the Christian life.

Salvation Also for the Faithful
Who Have Already Died (4:13–18)

After the warning and exhortation that Paul probably had to give in these, or similar, words in all the newly-founded communities, he now comes on to a teaching that is especially necessary for the Thessalonians. He has probably learned from Timothy that the community is sad and perhaps even confused. This arises from a faulty knowledge of their faith. Thus Paul has to present his exhortation against sadness in the form of a clarifying instruction.

No Pagan Sadness (4:13)

¹³*But we would not have you ignorant concerning those who are asleep, that you may not grieve as others do who have no hope.*

A life without hope is a sad life. If someone does not believe in a world beyond the grave, he must hope for a better future on earth, for man lives on hope. He cannot live without it; he becomes sad, whether he wants to admit his sadness or not. But sadness paralyzes a person's vital forces, or makes him behave wildly (cf. 4:11; 2 Thess. 3:11), in order to dull the secret sense of sadness. But the two things are equally dangerous for a Christian: a false passivity that lets everything happen, and a wild activity that brings confusion. Faith knows about the glorious future. Even at the grave the Christian still retains his hope. This takes from him all sadness, banishes all listlessness, and destroys the impulse to meaningless activity.

The Teaching as a Consequence of Faith in Christ (4:14)

¹⁴*For since we [truly] believe that Jesus died and rose again, even so, through Jesus, God will bring with him those who have fallen asleep.*

Man does not simply " have " a body that he thinks he can do without and without which he probably even imagines he might live better; rather, man lives bodily with all his senses. He is bodily determined through and through. A disembodied life of the soul after death did not seem to the man of antiquity a full human life, but resembled more a twilight sleep. That is why both Jews and Christians rightly hope for the full salvation of bodily resurrection and a new creation.

But how will this be? We can only point to Christ: we shall resemble the risen Lord. We await from heaven " the Lord Jesus Christ, who will change our lowly body to be like his glorious body, by power which enables him to subject all things to himself " (Phil. 3:20f.). Then creation is freed from its " bondage to decay " (Rom. 8:21); we have a " spiritual body " filled and transfigured by the Holy Spirit (1 Cor. 15:44); then our body also has its " redemption " (Rom. 8:23). " For creation waits with eager longing for the revealing of the sons of God " (Rom. 8:19). Whoever believes in God as creator also readily believes that God can create the world anew and better. He knows that God will one day gloriously perfect creation. " And he who sat upon the throne said: ' Behold, I make all things new ' " (Rev. 21:5). At the end there will be " a new heaven and a new earth " (Rev. 21:1).

But Christ is the " first fruit of those who have fallen asleep " (1 Cor. 15:20). The general resurrection of the dead has already begun with the resurrection of Christ. But not only that: the resurrected Christ is also the reason for our resurrection. All who are " dead in Christ " (4:16) " in Christ shall all be made alive . . . Christ the first fruits, then at his coming those who belong to Christ " (1 Cor. 15:22f.). It is Christ in and through whom our resurrection will be achieved.

As all salvation comes from him, so also will this last great saving deed. Even the dead will be able to march in the triumphal procession of Christ when the victorious end comes. We should not only look forward to eternal blessedness, but also to the day of the parousia. For this day will be the day of the victory of God. Then we shall see that God was right, and it will be a great triumphal day for Christ: " Then comes the end, when he delivers the kingdom to God the Father after destroying every rule and every authority of power. For he must reign until he has put all his enemies under his feet " (1 Cor. 15:24f.). Who would not look forward to this great feast of rejoicing? The hope of being able to experience that one day gives much comfort and help in times of difficulty.

The Justification of the Teaching from Revelation (4:15–17)

THE ARGUMENT FROM REVELATION (4:15)

[15]*For this we declare to you by the word of the Lord, that we who are alive, who are left until the coming of the Lord, shall not precede those who have fallen asleep.*

The " doctrines of . . . the resurrection of the dead, and eternal judgment " were, according to the Epistle to the Hebrews (6:2), among the elementary points of missionary preaching. That the dead are resurrected in order to be judged with the living will also have been mentioned by Paul in Thessalonica. But Paul's preaching was above all the preaching of salvation, and he had taught the Thessalonians to set their whole hope on the imminent parousia of the Lord (1:9f.; cf. Phil. 3:20). But now some new Christian converts had died in the community. Would not these also be able to celebrate the great festivity? Apparently, the Thessalonians had a wrong idea of the succession of events. They thought that the resurrection of the dead would not take place until just before the judgment and in order for them to be judged, that is after the parousia of Christ. Paul had to explain—and he appeals to the authority of the Lord in doing so—that the resurrection of the dead does not take place only for the judgment. If baptized Christians died before the coming of Christ, they are resurrected in time to be able to join in the great celebration.

A FREE RECOUNTING OF THE WORDS OF REVELATION (4:16–17)

[16]*For the Lord himself will descend from heaven with the cry of command, with the archangel's call, and with the sound of the trumpet of God. And the dead in Christ will rise first;* [17a]*then we who are alive, who are left, shall be called up together with them in the clouds to meet the Lord in the air; . . .*

If the fear of the Thessalonians is to be quieted, Paul must paint a picture of the right succession of the coming events. How will it be possible for the dead to share in the triumphal procession of Christ? Paul seeks to explain this. God will give the word of command that will put an end to all history and introduce the eschatological events. For " of that day or that hour no one knows, not even the angels in heaven, nor the Son, but only the Father " (Mk. 13:32). All has been determined in the plan of the Father, and the hour of the end remains hidden in the depth of his holy will.

But if the hour is there and God has given his command, the archangel Michael will summon the heavenly hosts, the retinue of the Lord (cf. 3:13), and a trumpet signal will give the sign. Then the voice of the angel and the trumpet signal will not only resound through the spaces of heaven, but penetrate to the graves of the dead beneath on the earth. The rousing call of the angel and the signal for the new beginning are intended for them also. Together with those who are still alive, they will be mightily summoned to meet the Lord. Then the great celebration begins. No image and no conception are adequate to represent this. The Lord will " deliver us from the wrath to come " (1:10), that will now come upon the world, " when the Lord Jesus is revealed from heaven with his mighty angels in flaming fire, inflicting vengeance upon those who do not know God and upon those who do not obey the gospel of our Lord Jesus " (2 Thess. 1:7f.). That is why the meeting cannot take place on the earth. The wrath that will then break upon the unbelieving world will not touch believers, for they will be snatched away, taken to Christ. Thus from Jesus we may not only hope for the forgiveness of sins, but also preservation from punishment and from final damnation.

All ideas are inadequate here: whoever is taken to Christ passes into the world beyond and the mode of being in which Christ is at home. We must probably understand this " removal " as a transformation. Like those who have been resurrected, those who are still alive are taken to Christ and thus passed into another mode of being. This world of Christ can be described only by the image of " air ". It is not the " clouds " that take one to Christ: what is meant is the sphere beyond the earthly world, in which other laws of existence reign than those of our creation. One cannot enter this world of Christ without being transformed, as Paul later explicitly says, but even here indicates: " We shall not all sleep, but we shall all be changed, in a moment, in the twinkling of an eye, at the last trumpet " (1 Cor. 15 : 1f.). The world of Christ is another world from ours here below. Here on earth we are still very apart from him. We must become different if we want finally to meet him. A great transformation is necessary.

17b. . . *and so we shall always be with the Lord.*

We learn nothing about the terrible end of the world and of sin, nor anything about the new world and life in it. The union of Christ with those who believe in him is the goal of history. When this goal has been reached, nothing else is worth mentioning. With Christ all things are given to us (Rom. 8 : 32). Then we shall live forever in union with Christ. For Christ is all blessedness. To be " with him " is the fulfillment and the whole of happiness; " exclusion from the presence of the Lord " is, on the other hand, " eternal destruction " (2 Thess. 1 : 9). But to have that goal before one's eyes is the only comfort of this world that can make the suffering of this life bearable. If we see this goal, then we are tempted to rejoice: " Our commonwealth is in heaven " (Phil. 3 : 20). And if we think further and deeper, we can even say: "[Our] life is hidden with Christ in God. When Christ who is our life appears, then [we] also will appear with him in glory " (Col. 3 : 4).

Final Exhortation (4 :18)

18*Therefore, comfort one another with these words.*

There is comfort in the words of Paul because they give hope for the future. It is important that Christians comfort one another. They must show one another that the situation is not hopeless, that there is a future for them. Thus light comes into their lives, and the darkness that obscures their eyes and makes them sad departs.

The Demands of the Hour (5:1–11)

The undercurrent of the expectation of the end runs through the whole letter. But orientation towards the coming of Christ has consequences for the Christian life. Despite all the uncertainty about the end, one thing is certain: " Of that day or that hour no one knows " (Mk. 13:32). Hence no one can say: " My master is delayed " (Mt. 24:48). Thus vigilance is what the time demands. Nor can anyone, on the other hand, say: " The day of the Lord has come " (2 Thess. 2:2). Thus sobriety is also what the time demands.

Knowledge of the Uncertainty of the End (5:1–3)

5:1But as to the times and the seasons, brethren, you have no need to have anything written to you. 2For you yourself know well that the day of the Lord will come like a thief in the night.

" If the householder had known at what hour the thief was coming, he would have been awake and would not have left his house to be broken into " (Lk. 12:9). But that is just the point: a thief always comes unexpectedly. Thus it will be also with the coming of Christ. We have one piece of certain knowledge about the time of the end, but it is knowledge that can easily be forgotten: we know, without needing further instruction, that the Lord will come with unexpected suddenness. No one knows when, but he can come any day. The uncertainty of the hour is all the certainty we have. We have to endure in this certainty and take it seriously.

³When people say : " There is peace and security," then sudden destruction will come upon them as travail comes upon a woman with child, and there will be no escape.

For those who live without care in peace and security, the day of the Lord will come with sudden terror. It will overwhelm them like destruction, great suffering from which there is no escape. For the Son of man will come when it is as in the days of Noah: " They ate, they drank, they married . . . ," and in the days of Lot: " They ate, they drank, they bought, they sold, they planted, they built . . ." (cf. Lk. 17:26–30). Then it will be for many of us as for the fool who said to himself: " Soul, you have ample goods laid up for many years; take your ease, eat, drink, be merry " (Lk. 12:16–20). We are warned against living carelessly in this kind of " peace " and against wrapping ourselves in this kind of " security." But the grace that lies in the uncertainty of the hour is the summons to be always ready. To be ever ready is the wisdom that the time demands.

The New Condition as the Sons of Light (5:4–5a)

⁴But you are not in darkness, brethren, for that day to surprise you like a thief. ⁵ᵃFor you are all sons of light and sons of the day; . . .

In the south the brightness of day comes very suddenly. So it will be also with the day of the Lord. In the dark earthly night Christians are already marked by the light of the coming day of Christ. They already have something of the light of Christ, of the coming day of God, about them. Whoever lives in the light becomes himself light. God " has delivered us from the dominion of darkness and transferred us to the kingdom of his beloved Son " (Col. 1:13). Thus Paul can later say more clearly: " Once you were darkness, but now you are light in the Lord; walk as children of light " (Eph. 5:8). But those around whom, as sons of light and sons of day, the light of the coming Lord already plays, and whose lives yearn for him in eager expectation, cannot be surprised by the end and be found unprepared. To live in the light means, above all, to be wakeful and sober and looking for what is to come. But without this light of hope, life falls back into the blind darkness of this world, in which one gives way to the " unfruitful works of darkness " (Eph. 5:11).

The Moral Consequences (5:5b–8)

VIGILANCE AND SOBRIETY (5:5b–8a)

⁵ᵇ*We are not of the night or of darkness.* ⁶*So then let us not sleep, as others do, but let us keep awake and be sober.*

If one knows nothing of the day of Christ, he lives in the dark- ness and like a man asleep. Asleep and dreaming, unbelievers never make contact with actual reality. A man who knows nothing of the end of the world and the return of Christ cannot know the world either. Vigilance is the demand of the morning hour. Whoever has been touched by the light of the coming Lord is awakened and called to be wholly awake. Whoever looks out in faith for the coming Lord remains awake and can take the world soberly as it is. If a man knows what the goal of creation and history is, he is able to act correctly in accordance with creation and history. Whoever knows the goal of his life can make the right decisions because he sees soberly the most important fact about his life. The ever-readiness that makes us watchful and sober is thus for Christians the basic demand of the hour in which we live.

⁷For those who sleep sleep at night, and those who get drunk are drunk at night. ⁸ᵃBut, since we belong to the day, let us be sober . . .

In the ancient world feasts were generally held at night; it was not so easy to get drunk in the daytime. The day demands sobriety: " Let us conduct ourselves becomingly as in the day, not in reveling and drunkenness, not in debauchery and licentiousness, not in quarreling and jealousy . . ." (Rom. 13:13). A good picture of wild ancient symposia! But here Paul is thinking of another kind of sobriety. " Sober " men see things objectively, as they are. They do not chase after fantasies or become intoxicated by idols. If a man knows Christ, he does not fall victim to these. He is protected against an idealism that obscures and confuses the world and is far from reality. Whoever knows Christ, the reality of all realities, always remains a sober realist.

The Need for Armor (5:8b)

⁸ᵇ. . . and put on the breastplate of faith and love, and for a helmet the hope of salvation.

The daytime also requires proper clothing: " Lo, I am coming like a thief! Blessed is he who is awake, keeping his garments . . ." (Rev. 16:15). But it is not enough to be clothed and girt. It is a time of battle, and therefore we need weapons, for " the night is far gone, the day is at hand. Let us then cast off the works of darkness and put on the armor of light " (Rom. 13:12). " Put on the whole armor of God, that you may be able to stand against the wiles of the devil. For we are not contending against flesh and blood . . . Take the whole armor of God, that you may be able to withstand in the evil day " (Eph. 6:11ff.).

In times of oppression we need the protection of armor and helmet. A community under persecution must protect itself. But what gives steadfastness, solidity, and protection to an oppressed and endangered community? We already know what Paul considers the most important thing in the life of the community: faith and love (3:6.10.12), but especially hope (1:10; 4:13). Where there is a living, loving faith, there men are well protected with strong armor that resists all attacks. Love has its firm strength (3:12f.). And whoever is looking out for the Lord and his salvation holds his head towards the light of the Lord; this flows round him and protects his head like a firm helmet. In times of trouble nothing is important but love, faith, and hope (cf. 1:3).

The Reason for the Exhortation (5:9–10)

⁹*For God has not destined us for wrath, but to obtain salvation through our Lord Jesus Christ,* ¹⁰ᵃ *who died for us . . .*

Christians do not need to fear the wrath of God's judgment at the end of time, because the returning Lord will snatch them from it (1:10) and take them wonderfully to himself (4:17).

Christians know that God's judgment can also come upon them, "for the time has come for judgment to begin with the household of God" (1 Pet. 4:17). But if one lives in loving faith and hopes for the Lord, he will not experience the wrath of God's judgment as eternal damnation. Christians may have great confidence that they will be saved at the end. They may assume that they are intended for salvation (cf. 1:4; 2:12). This gives a serene confidence that cannot be shaken by any earthly disaster.

What is such confidence based on? It is undoubtedly connected with the fact that we live in faith, love, and hope, armed, sober, and watchful (5:1-8). But this confidence does not trust in itself, but only in Christ. It is he who will save us when he comes and brings us salvation. And how do we know this? We know his love for us, for he has given his life for us, has died for us. "Who is to condemn [us]? Is it Christ Jesus, who died [for us], yet, who was raised from the dead, who is [now] at the right hand of God, who indeed intercedes for us?" (Rom. 8:34). Our confidence of being saved is based on a firm foundation: on the love of Christ. He who has died for us will undoubtedly continue to do everything to save us.

If one has understood the love of Jesus unto death, this will become the whole content of his life: "And the life I now live in the flesh I live by faith in the Son of God, who loved me and gave himself for me" (Gal. 2:20).

[10b]. . . *so that whether we wake or sleep we might* [*soon*] *live with him.*

Paul is looking back to 4:13-18: those Christians who have already died suffer no disadvantage and are not excluded from salvation. But in what does eternal salvation consist? In a life with Christ (4:14.17), in the closest possible connection and communion with Christ. He is heaven; he is life. And eternal bliss consists in communion with him. It is not necessary to say more about the coming salvation to someone whose whole love is Christ.

Final Exhortation (5:11)

¹¹*Therefore, encourage one another and build one another up, just as you are [already] doing.*

The church is built up primarily by the good word. " According to the commission of God given to me, like a skilled master builder I laid a foundation, and another man is building upon it. Let each man take care how he builds upon it . . . The fire will test what sort of work each one has done " (1 Cor. 3:10–13). The church cannot be built up through a word that is " hay " or " straw." There are words that are empty and discourses that tear down and leave ruins behind them. But the word should build up (cf. 1 Cor. 14), be of use (Mt. 12:36f.). It is comforting words that are able to build up (cf. 3:2). But those words are comforting that are able to awaken hope and give confidence in the eternal future. Christians live on such words of hope. One should tell the other and he yet another what awaits us. If this happens in a community, then truly that community is being built up as the house of God.

To consider the coming salvation gives comfort (cf. 4:13, 18). The promise of an eternal communion of love with Christ raises us up when we are weary and downcast. " If we look up

and raise [our] heads " (Lk. 21:28) in this expectation, our
heads are protected from all the arrows of despair and the
poison of hopelessness, with which the Evil One constantly
seeks to paralyze the life of faith and of love.

Christian Life in Community (5:12–22)

In this section a mirror is held up to the community. It must take
account of five things if the life of the community is to remain
healthy. The soul of community life is brotherly love (4:9f.); in all
questions it helps one to find the right solution.

Loving Harmony (5:12–13)

*12But we beseech you, brethren, to respect those who labor
among you and are over you in the Lord and admonish you,
13and to esteem them very highly in love because of their work.
Be at peace among yourselves.*

There can be no community life without some people working
particularly hard and conducting the affairs of the community.
Thus there were also in Thessalonica men who labored greatly
for the others; they were concerned about everything and were
pastorally involved with the brethren in a special way. They
talked to them, warned them and admonished them. We think
particularly of leaders of the community, whether appointed by
Paul himself before his flight or by Timothy on his commission.
This kind of work for the community is something very great,
for in these " services " it is the Lord himself who is at work;
they are " gifts of grace," in which the Spirit is active,

" powers," in which the power of God takes effect (1 Cor.
12:4ff.). Whenever a community has this kind of service within
it, powerful and worked by grace, the Lord himself is at work.
Whether such men have an official status or not, they always
have a high authority given them by the Lord. This work is
to be regarded with gratitude and respect because it takes place
" in the Lord." We should be aware of when someone is thus
working " in the Lord," of where there is a service that we
must estimate highly because it is done " in the Lord."

A Christian community is a brotherhood. Life in it is regulated
by love of the brethren (cf. 3:12; 4:9f.; 5:15). But love knows
that it must subordinate itself and to whom it must subordinate itself. In love one person is " subject to . . . another
out of reverence for Christ " (Eph. 5:21). Thus there can be
no quarreling, and peace is preserved. In love, which everywhere seeks unity, much is settled automatically.

Patience with the Weaker Brethren (5:14)

[14a] *And we exhort you, brethren, admonish the idle, encourage
the fainthearted, help the weak, . . .*

The Apostle's exhortation to pastoral concern for the idle,
fainthearted, and weak is directed not only to the leading men
in the community, but (as in 5:11) to all the brethren, all the
members of the community. After all, the community is like
one family, a pastoral unit in which everyone is responsible for
the salvation of the others. All the particular services and works
of a community must be set within the total structure of the
spiritual life of the community, in which everyone serves and
works in his own way.

First of all, those who are idle and live disorderly lives have to be admonished; for in Thessalonica as in any community there are those who do not participate sufficiently in the life of the community and are also lax in their moral life. Where in a community there is a lively love of the brethren, sin is overcome in mutual aid (cf. the example of 2 Thess. 3:6–15). One is concerned for the other, and all grow together. All official penance of the church is set within the framework of such fraternal endeavors; it is based on this spiritual brotherhood.

The life of the faithful who are waiting for the coming of the Lord is a life in the Spirit of the Lord, it is unusually gay and serene. Wherever a brother lacks this peaceful, joyous, and hopeful vitality and is fainthearted, he must be encouraged. Certainly, this requires gifts of the Spirit which are able to arouse emotions of confidence and joy in men's hearts (cf. 3:2f.).

Finally, there are brethren of a third kind in a community who need help: the weak, those who constantly need instruction and explanation, help and support, so that they are able to live the life of the community to its full extent and its full depth. In constant and unflagging love the weak should be looked after day by day. They must always be taken into consideration; the " strong " should not want to determine the faith and style of life of the community according to their own wishes. " We who are strong [in our conscience] ought to bear with the failings of the weak, and not to please ourselves; let each of us please his neighbor for his good, to edify him " (Rom. 15:1f.).

[14b]. . . *be patient with them all.*

This exhortation sounds like a summary. The early Christian communities were brotherhoods with a largely common life.

To live in community, however, means to bear with one another, to have patience with one's brother, to be ready to start over and over again with him without becoming impatient and giving up the community. It is necessary to be long-suffering if one is to live together in brotherhood with the idle, the fainthearted, and the weak. It is necessary to forbear one another in love (Eph. 4:2). Paul sees soberly and realistically. The idle, the fainthearted, the weak all require patience. But it is love that makes us patient (1 Cor. 13:4).

The Conquest of Evil in Love (5:51)

[15]*See that none of you repays evil for evil, but always seek to do good to one another and to all.*

It is not only idleness, faintheartedness, and weakness in the brethren that constantly tries the patience of the brotherly love of the community. A special problem is presented by injustice, which can destroy love and destroy the community. Here brotherly love has to withstand its strongest test, here we need the exhortation: " Do not be overcome by evil but overcome evil with good " (Rom. 12:21), as the Lord commanded. Love can bear with the mistakes and the weaknesses of the brethren if it is patient. But if evil is directed against one's own person, patient long-suffering is not enough. There attack is the best means of defense. But love attacks by bringing about the good. It is concerned with what benefits the other person, with the true good of one's brother. Love receives injustice, takes it to its heart, transforms it, and then reacts with goodness. Only if brotherly love is able to do that can it build up brotherhood and bring about unity in the community.

But love cannot be contained within the limits of one community. It becomes love to all men (cf. 3:12). Love of one's neighbor is learned in the school of love of the brethren. " If possible, so far as it depends upon you, live peaceably with all " (Rom. 12:18). Nay more: we should be concerned for the well-being of our neighbor, even if he is not a Christian brother. This will to do good to the other person should not obtain only before the forum of the community, rather " take thought for what is noble in the sight of all " (Rom. 12:17b).

The Constant Worship of God (5 :16–18)

[16]*Rejoice always,* [17]*pray constantly,* [18]*give thanks in all circumstances; for this is the will of God in Christ Jesus for you.*

It is not by chance that these three exhortations come so close together. Constant joy, constant prayer, and gratitude in all circumstances are flowers that all grow from the same root: from the Spirit of God in us, which continually, without interruption, and in every situation causes our soul to be with God. The world with all its evils is not such that one could always rejoice; there is also suffering. The necessities of life do not really permit constant prayer, and the many unpleasant experiences of our days are not always of a nature to rouse gratitude in our hearts. But the Christian who lives in the Spirit of God is not living only this earthly life; he is living a spiritual life. This has the power of taking into itself his earthly life and transforming it into the worship of God like a pure sacrificial fire. What is the will of God in a new Christian order of life? No longer, as in the Old Testament, the fulfillment of the law, but sanctification (4:3). But this culminates in a spiritual life of a kind that is constant joyful thanksgiving. It is important for men who are striving for salvation to experience what the will of God really is. This is stated here in concise terms: a life of constant joy, incessant prayer, and total thanksgiving.

The life of the early Christian community took place largely in the community assembly, where one listened to the word of God at the evening love-feast and celebrated the Eucharist with prayer (Acts 2:42). This is the root of all Christian life, but it is also its climax. Here it is especially important to have " glad and generous hearts " (Acts 2:46). When the community comes together, the keynote for the assembly, for as long as it lasts, should be joy. And common prayer should fill the hours, but especially the prayer of thanksgiving that culminates in the solemn prayer of the Eucharist. " Be filled with the Spirit, addressing one another in psalms and hymns and spiritual songs, singing and making melody to the Lord with all your heart, always and for everything giving thanks in the name of our Lord Jesus Christ to God the Father " (Eph. 5:18ff.). The new life in the Holy Spirit impels people to assemble in community and expresses itself in it, but it also lives from the assembly of the community as its source. It is the school of a life in the Holy Spirit, in constant joy and incessant, grateful prayer.

Life in the Spirit (5:19–22)

[19]*Do not quench the Spirit,* [20]*do not despise prophesying* . . .

In contrast to Corinth, where Paul had to bring order into overflowing charisms, the gifts of the Spirit do not seem to have been exactly overvalued in Thessalonica. The community of Thessalonica was probably not yet " aglow with the Spirit " (Rom. 12:11). The community is still young, and the spiritual life only in its beginnings. But we may assume that there were in Thessalonica individual mystic graces of prayer which expressed themselves ecstatically as " the gift of tongues." The new Christian converts, however, did not yet know how to evaluate properly these and other gifts of the Spirit.

Paul could have written here also: " Earnestly desire the spiritual gifts, especially that you may prophesy " (1 Cor. 14:1). Christians are to place particular value on the gift of prophecy. Its task is by no means simply the illumination of the future, for " he who prophesies edifies the church " (1 Cor. 14:4) and " speaks to men for their upbuilding and encouragement and consolation " (14:3), and that frequently on the basis of a special revelation (1 Cor. 14:30). This kind of prophet is also able to " convict " sinners in the Holy Spirit, " call them to account," and " disclose the secrets of their hearts " (1 Cor. 14:25). The church is built not only on the foundations of the apostles, but also on that of the prophets (Eph. 2:20). In the church today there are no longer any apostles, but there are " successors of the apostles." Similarly, there are no longer today the early Christian prophets (who were still receivers of revelation), but simply Christians who succeed them, having the Holy Spirit in a particular way. But where the prophetic spirit operates in the manner described above, there the church is built up in a particularly effective way. Hence the gifts of the Spirit should be valued within a Christian community.

[21]*But test everything; hold fast what is good;* [22]*abstain from every form of evil.*

The prophetic spirit speaks through the mediation of the minds of men. Thus everything that a prophet says should be tested to see whether it really comes from God. For a community must keep itself from evil, even if it appears in the form of utterance which comes from the Spirit. Christians have the gift of distinguishing between spirits. The Holy Spirit gives spiritual judgment to the believer. It is not the decisions of the apostolic teaching office that keep the church's life of faith sound, but also the spiritual judgment of the faithful, that is able to distinguish between good and bad. But our love must " abound more and more, with knowledge and all discernment, so that [we] may approve what is excellent " (Phil. 1:9f.), " what is the will of God " (Rom. 12:3). And this spiritual judgment is then able not only to know theoretically what is true and God's command, it is also able to know practically and concretely what is and what is not the will of God in any particular situation. The Holy Spirit must help Christians to distinguish between truth and error, to find the right thing to do in every historical situation, and discover the will of God.

Summing Up in a Final Exhortation (5:23-24)

[23a]*May the God of peace himself sanctify you wholly . . .*

We have already seen (4:3; cf. 5:18) that God's will is our sanctification. It is completely the work of God. This work of sanctification is not concluded with baptism; Paul knows that his Thessalonians are not perfect (cf. 3:10.12), and that even after baptism Christ must continue to do his sanctifying work in them (3:13). God must complete the work he has begun until the whole inadequate man is perfect.

[23b]*. . . and may your spirit and soul and body be kept sound and blameless at the coming of our Lord Jesus Christ.*

Concern for the constancy of the Thessalonians resounds continually through the lines of this letter (cf. especially 3:5-8).
The sanctifying work that God has performed in men remains
in danger, so much so that God himself must preserve his work.

First and foremost God must protect the gift of the Holy
Spirit, the new spiritual life that he has given us. If God does
this, then men will remain blameless in soul and body. The
weak man cannot continue blameless until his encounter with
the Lord, unless God strengthens his heart (3:13). Paul wishes
us something here that ought also to be our most fervent wish:
the gift of persistence to the end.

[24]*He who calls you is faithful, and he will do it.*

At the end God will call everyone to him. But this end is
already there; the call has gone out and is going out in this
very moment. That is why this moment in which we are living
is so important. Our life stands beneath the ultimate call of God.
God is calling us—through the mouth of his apostles—" into his
own kingdom and glory " (2:12). He who has heard this call
will no longer be able to get it out of his head; it will give him
no rest.

God is faithful; he is faithful, above all, to himself. What he
has begun he " will bring . . . to completion at the day of Jesus
Christ " (Phil. 1:6). This thought gives us confidence, great
trust, but it is the trust that is based on God alone (cf. 5:9f.).

The community is in danger: outside, oppression and persecution; inside, weakness—yet God will do it. This is the last
statement of the letter of the Apostle, filled with concern, but
sustained, from the first sentence to the last, by a great confidence.

THE CLOSE OF THE LETTER
(5:25–28)

THE CLOSE OF THE LETTER (5:25–28)

A Request to Be Remembered in Prayer (5:25)

25Brethren, pray for us.

This is the request of an apostle. The community is to help in his apostolic work (cf. 2 Thess. 3:1). Paul thought it important for the Thessalonians to remember him (3:6). But this finds its fullest form in remembrance in prayer, above all in commemoration of the common prayer in the worship of God. The communion of the church is confirmed in this prayerful commemoration. That is why he addresses them as " brethren " at the beginning of the sentence.

Intended for the Whole Community (5:26–27)

26Greet all the brethren with the holy kiss.

In the gentile communities of the apostolic period the custom arose of taking leave of one another after the common evening meal with the " holy kiss," the " kiss of love " (1 Pet. 5:14), an eloquent sign of brotherly love in the community.

The Christians called it the " holy " kiss to distinguish it, probably also because it communicated the gift of the Holy Spirit. This is particularly true when it is given to every brother, as here, as an apostolic commission. It is an effective grace-giving greeting. For if Christians are devoted to one another in true brotherly love, they are able to bestow rich graces on one another. Where Christians become one with one another, a contact is established through which the gifts of grace of the Holy Spirit can flow and become effective.

²⁷I adjure you by the Lord that this letter be read to all the brethren.

Paul wants his letter to be read publicly to the assembly of the community. Everyone is to hear it; he has not written a private letter. The apostolic message is intended to reach everyone, even today. The apostolic letters are to be read in public and in private. Through their inspired writings the apostles continue to live in the church in a quite special way. Through these writings of theirs they speak in the church to all ages and to everyone. The apostolic word must not fall silent in the Christian community.

A Blessing (5:28)

²⁸The grace of our Lord Jesus Christ be with you!

Paul takes his leave with a wish. Perhaps he had already done this at the end of the assemblies of the community. But an apostle not only wishes the grace of the Lord; he communicates it also. All the spiritual grace that the words of Paul have conveyed is here summed up again in this wish: " The grace of our Lord Jesus Christ be with you!" But we can be sure that Paul also desired Christians outside Thessalonica to read his letter. As members of the church we know that the grace-giving wish of the Apostle is intended for us also, who have now finished reading his letter.

The Second Epistle
to the Thessalonians

INTRODUCTION

Since Christ has come into this world, the last times are upon us. The powers of the kingdom of God, which are already at work, press towards their fulfillment. For the believer, his and history's goal is the new heaven and the new earth (Rev. 21:1). Jesus Christ has proclaimed the gospel of salvation and stated with all possible urgency that the dawn of the new age has already begun. The Christian must be sober and watchful in his faith.

It is in this age that the church which the Lord wants to bring to himself as his beloved bride lives. It passes through the world and does not lose sight of its goal, namely, being gathered together with Jesus Christ (2:1). Not all men believe the gospel of the coming kingdom of God in Christ (3:2). In spite of this and without giving itself over to heresies and false enthusiasms, the church must go its way calmly and watchfully. It must take the apostolic proclamation seriously and realize it. Every Christian community is the church at the place where it lives. But in a pagan environment there are dangers for the community. It can be misled and seduced away from sound doctrine, both by the false teachers of this "world" as also by false brethren (2 Cor. 11:26). Thus it is a duty of the Apostle to protect his communities from false doctrines and to counter abuses. The community of Thessalonica had made a good start. The Apostle was able to present them as a model, not only in Macedonia and Achaia, but everywhere (1 Thess. 1:8). But now he has heard that abuses have arisen in the community. Thus he feels himself obliged, as an apostle and pastor in the service of the Lord, to write the community a letter in which he is forced to discuss the false doctrines and the abuses.

1. Probably the attacks on the young Christian community had become more severe. The Jews in Thessalonica, who had sought to rouse the people and the leaders of the town against Paul (cf. Acts 17:13), had perhaps taken further steps against the community. Thus the Christians had to undergo suffering, persecution, and affliction. The Apostle has to tell his community that suffering and affliction are part of the Christian life. The Lord himself said: "Remember the word that I said to you, 'A servant is not greater than his master.' If they persecuted me, they will persecute you . . ." (Jn. 15:20). Christians are pilgrims and strangers in this world and have to bear much suffering. But they suffer for the sake of the kingdom of God. Faith and patience are the attitudes in which the Christian can withstand the assault of the world. The Apostle is able to say full of joy that he could boast to the other churches of God of the patience and faith of the Thessalonians (1:4).

But the suffering will come to an end. Christians must only not lose sight of their goal, and meet all their affliction. When the Lord Jesus Christ comes again, then the community will be able to celebrate its glorious victory (1:10). Then their oppressors will be punished (1:6). They have missed the moment, rejected the Lord Jesus Christ, and persecuted his disciples. That is why at the end of time they will meet with just judgment.

2. In great distress man longs for the end of the period of his sufferings. The community knows that when the Lord comes everything will be all right; every tear will be wiped away (Rev. 21:4), and Christians will be with the Lord for

ever, in unending joy (1 Thess. 4:17). In suffering and persecution the church can long more urgently for the return of
the Lord than in periods of calm. But at such times people
can appear who feel particularly illuminated or qualified. They
claim to have more exact knowledge concerning the return of
the Lord. Through this, extravagant imaginings, heresies, and
an uncritical attitude can spring up in the community.

The church, in its expectation of the Lord, can be threatened
by two wrong attitudes: a cosiness, in which the immediately
imminent coming of the Lord is no longer taken seriously, or
an excited enthusiasm that pays no further regard to the word
of the Lord: " Take heed, watch; for you do not know when
the time will come " (Mk. 13:33).

In his First Epistle to the Thessalonians Paul had to counter
the first wrong attitude. A self-satisfied attitude of false security
and superficial peace can spring up, even within the church.
" When people say: ' There is peace and security,' then sudden
destruction will come upon them as travail comes upon a woman
with child, and there will be no escape " (1 Thess. 5:3).

In the Second Epistle to the Thessalonians Paul has to attack
the other attitude. Either through a false prophet or some mis-
interpretation of the apostolic proclamation or a forged letter
from Paul (2:2), great excitement had arisen in the community.
The reason for it is the statement that the day of the Lord had
already arrived.

Paul had to oppose this opinion firmly, because it was dangerous for a healthy community life and the life of faith. Paul
dampens the enthusiasm of these visionaries by telling them to
remember his preaching. He had told them very clearly that
before the final appearance of the Lord events would occur in
which faith would be put to the test. The anti-Christ will

appear. The church will have to live in great affliction, and
many will fall away (2:3). With pretended wonders and great
signs of power the anti-Christ will gain great influence over
those who are lost (2:9). The faithful will have to wage a tough
battle against lies and seduction. Those who are not anchored
firmly in their faith will believe the lies. Through this they are
already judged (2:11f.). Thus there is no ground for excessive
joy or enthusiasm. The hard reality must be seen and accepted.
To stand firm in faith and hold firm to the oral and written
traditions that the community has received from Paul: that is
what the time demands.

The anti-Christ will in his time be destroyed by the Lord
Jesus, with the breath of his mouth (2:8). He is part of the
mighty conduct of history by God and must appear and dis-
appear at the given time. Everything stands in the power of
God alone. Despite the suffering that is still to come, and despite
all the struggles and persecutions, the true Christians will emerge
at the end as victors and be taken into the glory of God (1:10).
Although he throws cold water on their enthusiasm, Paul seeks
to comfort and encourage his community. But now Christians
must wait in the obedience of faith and in joyful hope for the
hour determined by God, without letting themselves be confused
by any fantastic imaginings.

3. Apart from these fundamental admonitions, Paul has also
to counter very energetically an abuse in the community. There
are idlers who want to live at the expense of members of the
community. They hang around and are no good to anybody.
We do not know exactly why this abuse had arisen in the
community. A likely explanation is that some people in the
community gave up their work because they expected the return
of the Lord in the immediate future. In their opinion it was

pointless to go on working. But possibly there were also some who had been converted, but fallen back into their earlier laziness. For a free Greek it was a matter for shame to have to work. But perhaps some Christians also wanted to live the comfortable life of a rich town resident at the cost of the community.

Paul had to intervene with his whole apostolic authority in order to correct these people. The idlers can easily arouse discontent in the community. Probably they even appeal to the Christian love of one's neighbor and thus challenge the kindhearted.

Those members of the community who worked hard and quietly could be disappointed by their brothers and sisters and come to think that someone who practices Christian love is simply exploited. They could become bitter and give up.

Paul reprimands the idlers. He points to his own example. When he was in Thessalonica, he had worked day and night so as not to have to bother anyone (3:7f.). He did this for two reasons, although, as the servant of the word, he could have claimed his right to hospitality (2:9). He wanted to manifest his pure intention and avoid giving the impression that he wanted to make money out of the proclamation of the gospel of Christ. Moreover, he did not want to make his presence an additional burden to the poor people of Thessalonica. Therefore, he had worked among them. His exhortations culminated in the clear instruction: " If any one will not work, let him not eat " (3:10).

But despite these abuses the good should not grow tired of doing good (3:13). It is only through love that the community of Christ will be believed in by the world. Therefore, despite all the setbacks, Christians must constantly maintain this basic

Christian attitude. The idlers must be admonished, if necessary, and even avoided (3:14); but they are and remain brethren. Enmity in the community would hinder the spread of the gospel and harm the life of the church (3:14f.).

The apostle Paul wrote his Second Epistle to the Thessalonians from Corinth, shortly after his First Epistle to them. This letter gives us a living picture of the community life of the early church. But it also shows us that at any time in the church abuses can arise. To counter them is the common task of the leaders of the church and of the faithful, who live in the world, watchful and sober, awaiting the Lord Jesus Christ.

OUTLINE

The Opening of the Letter (1 : 1–2)

THE LETTERHEAD (1 : 1–2)

   I. The senders and the recipients (1 : 1)

  II. The greeting (1 : 2)

The Body of the Letter (1 : 3—3 : 16)

EXPLANATION OF THE SITUATION (1 : 3–12)

   I. Thanksgiving (1 : 3–4)

  II. Strengthening (1 : 5–10)

     1. Suffering as a sign of election (1 : 5)

     2. The new age and the return of the Lord (1 : 6–8)

     3. The eternal punishment of the godless (1 : 9)

     4. The glorification of the Lord at the end of time (1 : 10)

III. Intercession (1 : 11–12)

THE MAIN CONCERNS OF THE LETTER (2 : 1—3 : 16)

   I. Warning against an error about the return of Christ (2 : 1–12)

     1. An urgent request (2 : 1–2)

     2. A reminder about the coming of the anti-Christ (2 : 3–5)

     3. Necessary additional teaching (2 : 6–12)

       a) The full revelation of the anti-Christ is still to come (2 : 6–7)

       b) The final appearance and destruction of the anti-Christ (2 : 8)

       c) The consequences for non-believers (2 : 9–12)

II. The right spirit of faith (2:13—3:5)
   1. Thanksgiving for the election of the brethren (2:13-14)
   2. Exhortation to steadfastness (2:15-17)
   3. A request for intercession (3:1-2)
   4. Renewed strengthening in faith (3:3-5)

III. Idleness and laziness in the community (3:6-16)
   1. Idle fellow Christians should be shunned (3:6)
   2. The apostolic example (3:7-9)
   3. A reminder of an earlier exhortation concerning idleness (3:10-12)
   4. Some instructions for the whole community (3:13-15)
   5. A prayer for peace (3:16)

The Close of the Letter (3:17-18)
THE CLOSE OF THE LETTER (3:17-18)
  I. Paul's greeting in his own handwriting (3:17)
  II. The grace (3:18)

THE OPENING OF THE LETTER
(1:1–2)

THE LETTERHEAD (1:1–2)

The Senders and the Recipients (1:1)

^{1a}*Paul, Silvanus, and Timothy . . .*

In the life of the church there is to be no divisive hierarchy.
All the faithful are called to the freedom of the children of God.
Certainly, there are differences in responsibility and in tasks;
but there is to be no quarreling about positions and honors.
The Lord said to his disciples: " You are not to be called
Rabbi, for you have one teacher, and you are all brethren "
(Mt. 23:8).

It is in this spirit that Paul and his fellow workers greet the
brethren and sisters of Thessalonica. The letter indicates the
brotherly attitude among the servants of the word by emphasiz-
ing the conjunction " and ": Paul *and* Silvanus *and* Timothy,
united to one another in fraternal love, greet the community.
The concern of the Apostle is directed towards the life of the
community. Thus an office in the church is not a position of
honor, since its holder has to work humbly and fervently for
the obedience of the little flock.

Silvanus and Timothy are two proven assistants of the Apostle
Paul. In their apostolic work they have experienced much joy
and suffering. Paul and Silvanus were together in captivity.
Because of their confession of Christ they had received many
beatings. In prison they had prayed at midnight and sung

praises to God. The Lord had freed them from their captivity in a wonderful way (cf. Acts 16: 19–30). Experiences in which the Lord reveals his power unite the disciples of the Lord.

Timothy is a pupil of Paul. The Apostle was able to rely on him. He often praised him and offered him as an example to the churches. " I hope in the Lord Jesus to send Timothy to you soon, so that I may be cheered by news of you. I have no one like him, who will be genuinely anxious for your welfare. They all look after their own interests, not those of Jesus Christ. But Timothy's worth you know, how as a son with his father he has served with me in the gospel " (Phil. 2: 19–22). In these recommendations to the community in Philippi the Apostle shows the deep friendship that unites him with Timothy.

Silvanus and Timothy have preached the gospel together, as commanded by the Apostle. They were together in Macedonia in order to preach Christ there (Acts 18:5). After that they were again together with the Apostle in Corinth.

He who gives witness for Christ does not remain alone. He will find brothers and sisters who are also seized by the power of the word of God. Thus a new brotherhood springs up on the basis of Christ's commission: " Go, therefore, and make disciples of all nations " (Mt. 28: 19). Three men greet the community which, in following Christ, has received the assistance and the strength of the Lord. Thus they are able and seek to establish the community on the firm foundation of a sound faith, free from fantasy and empty heresies.

1b. . . To the church of the Thessalonians [which lives] in God our Father and the Lord Jesus Christ : . . .

The recipient of the letter is the " church " in Thessalonica.

Every community, however poor and small, is the church of Jesus Christ. The men of a particular town discover through a Christian community in their place what the church is.

The Christian community in a town is sharply differentiated from the social and civic community by its presence in God our Father and the Lord Jesus Christ. Probably the writers of the letter are visualizing the community gathered for the worship of God. This provides the context in which the faithful can hear the word of God in a concentrated and direct way, because Christ himself speaks through the word of the apostles. They come together in the liturgical assembly in order to hear the gospel and to be strengthened for life in the world.

The one Father, our Father, unites all the churches and all Christians with one another. Everywhere in the world there are living children of God who can say and pray " Our Father." The Apostle emphasizes this fact in order to testify to his union with the community in God our Father and the Lord Jesus Christ.

The Greeting (1:2)

²Grace to you and peace from God the Father and the Lord Jesus Christ.

The new life in God results in two forms and customs of living. Paul is not satisfied with the normal form of greeting in which Greeks wished one another joy. Hence he wishes the community that saving good from which all goodness depends. When they greet one another people wish one another " all good things." God has redeemed us through Jesus Christ and made us new creatures. " For once you were darkness, but now you are light in the Lord " (Eph. 5:8). This is achieved by grace. It makes us new men, Christ's perfume in the world. The Christian should be attractive, loving, and charming. Thus Paul first wishes the community this good, from which all other good follows.

Peace was what the peoples always longed for. The Israelites believed that God would give peace at the end of time. Peace is perfect harmony among all men. God's blessing will rest on the community of men, and they will be able to develop fully according to their own particular natures. Peace is constantly shattered by injustice and lack of love. Men know that peace is their greatest joy, and yet they are unable to find their way to it by themselves.

With Christ the last times have come upon us. If someone approaches Christ, receives his gifts of grace, and shows himself worthy of them, he is able to receive true peace now and live in it. For it is true of Christ now that " he is our peace, who has made us both one, and has broken down the dividing wall of hostility " (Eph. 2:14). On the basis of the faith and love that a community receives through the grace of Christ, it is able to live today and here in inner peace, at least. That is why Christians should wish one another grace and peace.

Grace and peace which come from God the Father and the Lord Jesus Christ will also spread outside the community of the faithful, if they are themselves truly sons of peace and act accordingly. Then something of that perfect and comprehensive peace becomes visible that is promised as a gift of salvation at the end of time.

Again Paul mentions God the Father and the Lord Jesus Christ together. In this he is confessing Christ, the Son of God.

In the Old Testament men prayed to Yahweh, the Lord. We also pray to Christ the Lord. In the title " *Kyrios,*" which is later expanded in the liturgy to the cry " *Kyrie eleison* " the church confesses Christ, the Son of God. Through him and with him and in him it now honors the Father in heaven.

THE BODY OF THE LETTER
(1:3—3:16)

EXPLANATION OF THE SITUATION (1:3-12)

The community received the word of God, which they learned from Paul, not in a human way, but " in power and in the Holy Spirit and with full conviction " (1 Thess. 1:5). The community grew quietly, and was soon so strong that it was able to be a model for all the neighboring communities. But now this good beginning is in danger. The Jews in Thessalonica saw the new Christian community as a dangerous rival. They roused the people against the community and the apostles. Paul had experienced this enmity in Thessalonica in his own person, for his own people had stirred up the political authorities against him. " These men who have turned the world upside down have come here also, and Jason has received them; and they are all acting against the decrees of Caesar, saying that there is another king, Jesus " (Acts 17:6f.). Many Christians suffered the affliction and difficulties that come to those who follow Christ. For this reason Paul wants to give a word of explanation. The Christian is not safe from persecution. On the contrary, the tensions will be heightened. " You will be hated by all for my name's sake. But he who endures to the end will be saved " (Mk. 13:13). In these words the Lord himself had prophesied persecutions for his disciples. Thus affliction and ill treatment by men are no reason for being sad or losing heart, but rather they are grounds for joy. These experiences are a sign that the community is to become worthy of the kingdom of God. God is just. " On that day " he will punish the oppressors with oppression. So Paul is able to comfort the community and exhort them to be patient.

Thanksgiving (1:3-4)

[3a] *We are bound to give thanks to God always for you, brethren,
as is fitting, . . .*

Most of Paul's letters begin with joyful thanksgiving. He always
sees first the effects of the working of God's grace. It holds the
community together and enables it to be a testimony for
Christians and non-Christians. In faith he sees the working of
God who sustains his church and assists the apostles that he
uses as tools. Only after the praise of God's power in the
churches does Paul feel himself obliged to exhort and admonish.
But despite all the failures in some communities, the first thing
remains thanksgiving for the direction by God.

This thanksgiving is a matter of duty. Whoever sees with
open eyes and therefore understands must thank God for his
glorious guidance. This duty of thanksgiving is only right and
proper. As on a pair of scales the weights must correspond to
the wares, so the thanks of the community must correspond to
the mighty deeds of God. A man who would refuse the Lord
thanks for his work in the church and only complain would be
very ungrateful; for our thanks and praise of God can never
be equal to what God has done for us.

In the celebration of the Eucharist we find an echo of Paul's
words: " Let us give thanks to the Lord our God. It is right
and fitting. It is truly right and fitting and proper for our
salvation that we should at all times and in all places give
thanks to thee, Lord, holy Father, almighty everlasting God."

Thanksgiving and joy lead us to a deeper brotherhood. Thus
Paul addresses the community as " brethren." We must give

thanks because, through the love of God, which surpasses everything, we have become brothers and sisters, " a chosen race, a
royal priesthood, a holy nation " (1 Pet. 2:9).

[3b]. . . *because your faith is growing abundantly, and the love of
every one of you for one another is increasing.*

Paul was able to see how quickly Christian life could grow in
strength. Faith is not only holding on to revealed truth; it is
life that can grow and flourish, but also become weak and ill.
In faith the Christian experiences new life. His eyes are open
to the glory of God, and his ears hear the word of truth and
life. Thus faith must be nourished if it is to grow properly.
A man who hears the words of the Apostle " will be a good
minister of Christ Jesus, nourished on the words of the faith
and of the good doctrine " (1 Tim. 4:6). The flourishing of
faith in the community founded by Paul is the reason for the
Apostle's profound and joyful gratitude to the Lord.

The immediate result of a strong faith is living love. Faith
without love would be like the sun without warmth, an
impossibility. " If I have all faith, so as to remove mountains,
but have not love, I am nothing " (1 Cor. 13:2). The mark of
true discipleship is the love that comes from faith: " By this all
men will know that you are my disciples, if you have love for
one another " (Jn. 13:35).

Paul is particularly happy about love within the community.
The love of Christians for one another is an eloquent testimony
to faith for the world. In Jerusalem people began to take note
of the church because of the brotherly love that existed in the
Christian community. " They devoted themselves to the apostles'

teaching and [brotherly] fellowship . . . praising God and having favor with all the people. And the Lord added to their
number day by day those who were being saved " (Acts
2 : 42.47).

The Lord himself said that the love of his disciples for one
another was to be a sign for the world: " I in them and thou
in me that they may become perfectly one, so that the world
may know that thou hast sent me and hast loved them even
as thou hast loved me " (Jn. 17 : 23). The new life in faith and
love is the gift of the Father to his children, a ray of God's
light in the darkness of unbelief and sin. Praise and thanksgiving is the answer of the man who has received new life.

[4a] *Therefore, we ourselves boast of you in the churches of God . . .*

Paul's joy at the strong growth of the community is immediately
converted into the praise of God; but it can also edify other
churches. He goes on to say what he had experienced with the
Thessalonians. Through this the other churches are spurred
on and encouraged. The life of a good community has a stimu-
lating effect on neighboring communities. Paul does not disguise
out of any false modesty the missionary successes with the
Thessalonians. He knows only too well that it is the Lord that
gives the increase. To give reports of successes and happy experiences in the churches of God is a form of praise of God.
Only a man who sees the faith and the love of a community
as the work of Christ can testify to the power and grace of God
in the church.

[4b] *. . . for your steadfastness and faith in all your persecutions
and in the afflictions which you are enduring.*

Paul's praise is well-founded. The community has recently undergone much and bravely accepted the prophesied trials. The faith of the church always arouses opposition. Persecution and prison, contempt and poverty, ill treatment and ridicule are things that believers must accept from those who proudly and indifferently reject Christ. "All who desire to live a godly life in Christ Jesus will be persecuted, while evil men and impostors will go on from bad to worse, deceivers and deceived " (2 Tim. 3 : 12f.).

These sufferings are a test for the Christian. It is here that he must show whether he is ready to lose his life in order to find it (Mt. 10 : 39). If a Christian bears patiently the sufferings that come to him in this last time, they will redound to his credit in the great new beginning that is coming. Patience and steadfastness, however, are not the personal achievement of the Christian, but a great present of God. For this reason the Christian can remain obediently at his task, accepting the burden of his sufferings. He does not fall victim to the temptation to flee from death-bringing oppression, and he does not give up the struggle with the powers and principalities, for only " he who endures to the end will be saved " (Mt. 24 : 13).

Strengthening (1 : 5–10)

Despite great steadfastness, sufferings can also become a temptation if we cannot see any end to them. Paul, as a pastor, paints in sharp colors the picture of the end of the world, so that the community does not lose sight of its point of orientation, and in the sufferings of the present forget the goal of its journey: eternal joy with the Lord.

Suffering as a Sign of Election (1 :5)

⁵*This is evidence of the righteous judgment of God, that you may be made worthy of the kingdom of God, for which you are suffering.*

The judgment of God is beginning. In the purifying fire of suffering God is already dividing men up. At the end of history God will then make known his decision. All who persevere in faith and love will belong in the kingdom of God at the end of the world. Thus it is worth enduring in suffering, because the believer can see it as a testing period for being received into the kingdom of God. " If one suffers as a Christian, let him not be ashamed, but under that name let him glorify God. For the time has come for the judgment to begin with the household of God; and if it begins with us, what will be the end of those who do not obey the gospel of God?" (1 Pet. 4: 16f.).

The Lord told his disciples that he would have to suffer much in order to enter into his glory. These were hard words for the disciples of Jesus, and they never really wanted to believe them. Thus Paul also has to explain to his churches the necessity of suffering. This is unintelligible and irritating to a world that is not ready to be among " those who belong to Christ Jesus [and] have crucified the flesh with its passions and desires " (Gal. 5: 24). In the Acts of the Apostles Luke reports concerning the preaching of Paul and Barnabas among the new Christians of South Galatia that they had been " strengthening the souls of the disciples, exhorting them to continue in the faith, and saying that through many tribulations we must enter the kingdom of God " (Acts 14: 22).

The New Age and the Return of the Lord (1:6–8)

⁶Since indeed God deems it just to repay with affliction those who afflict you, ⁷ᵃand to grant rest with us to you who are afflicted, . . .

A secret and an open cause of distress for those who fear God is the question as to why the godless prosper and the godly suffer. The psalmist had already made the painful observation: " For I was envious of the arrogant, when I saw the prosperity of the wicked. For they have no pains; their bodies are round and sleek " (Ps. 73:3). But at the end of the psalm he recognizes the truth: " For lo, those who are far from thee shall perish; thou dost put an end to those who are false to thee. But for me it is good to be near God " (Ps. 73:27f.). " Do not be deceived; God is not mocked; for whatever man sows, that he will also reap " (Gal. 6:7). This will become clear at the end. The oppressors of the faithful will themselves suffer oppression. It will be suffering of a kind they never thought possible, for " it is a fearful thing to fall into the hands of the living God " (Heb. 10:31).

The punishment that the oppressors will undergo is not the punishment of a God that hits out blindly. They will only see that their godless attitude has made them incapable of the fellowship of God's love. But this will then be revealed as the ultimate significance of every human life. They have caused their own eternal damnation, since the separation from God that they have desired all their lives will now continue for all eternity. That will be their suffering. In eternal hopelessness they will look longingly for the love of God. Whereas those who " in hope . . . believed against hope " (Rom. 4:18) will experience the fulfillment of their hope to a degree they never suspected. In blessed communion with God they will be able to share in his joy and his glory. " What no eye has seen, nor ear heard, nor the heart of man conceived, God has prepared for those who love him " (1 Cor. 2:9).

Paul the pastor says: You will enjoy this peace together with us. The shepherd and the flock will sit down together with the Lord to the heavenly banquet and be able to share the joys with the great company of the chosen.

[7b]. . . *when the Lord Jesus is revealed from heaven with his mighty angels in flaming fire,* . . .

The revelation of the Lord at the Last Judgment will bring the fulfillment of hope. He will show himself in full power and make perfect his kingdom. Only in images of the human imagination is the believer able to form some impression of the coming event. Paul here uses images from the description of the Last Judgment found in the Old Testament. But the New Testament also depicts in sharp colors the scene of judgment at the return of Christ. All these pictures, however, serve only to underline one fact: The Lord will come with power. No man can gainsay him. God's will will then be done on earth as in heaven: on the new earth and in the new heaven.

" His mighty angels " are the good powers and forces that have protected and guided men throughout their history, and they will reveal themselves. They will gather the elect from the four corners of the earth (Mk. 13:27). The power and majesty of the Lord is emphasized by the great splendor of those with him. The flaming fire is a symbol of the relentless vengeance of God. Everything that does not withstand the fire is burned.

" For behold, the Lord will come in fire, and his chariots like
the wind storm, to render his anger in fury, and his rebuke
with flames of fire. For by fire will the Lord execute judgment "
(Is. 66:15f.). The author of Hebrews calls the faithful to thanksgiving and reverence for God, who has revealed to us how
dangerous the situation of the world is. " Therefore let us be
grateful for receiving a kingdom that cannot be shaken, and
thus let us offer to God acceptable worship, with reverence and
awe; for our God is a consuming fire " (Heb. 12:28f.).

God will carry out the judgment only indirectly. The Messiah
who proclaimed to men the good news of liberation from the
darkness of sin and error will also judge the sons of disobedience.

[8]*. . . inflicting vengeance upon those who do not know God and
upon those who do not obey the gospel of our Lord Jesus.*

The gospel of saving grace would have no meaning if there
were no damnation. If someone rejects God's offer of love, he
must expect punishment. He will never be able to receive his
love again. God will avenge himself on those who do not want
to know him. Paul is not here going into the question of
whether a man who has never heard anything of Christ can
be saved. He is concerned with the people who know exactly
what is at issue but reject the gospel of God and the Lord Jesus.
They do not want to repent and do penance but continue their
old style of life in the " desires of the flesh " (Gal. 5:16).

Two attitudes stand in the way of obedient faith: pride and
sin. Paul has often had to be a witness of this disobedience to
the gospel. In Athens he proclaimed to the philosophers the
gospel of Jesus Christ but they made fun of Paul: " ' What
would this babbler say?' . . . now when they heard of the

resurrection of the dead, some mocked; but others said: 'We will hear you again about this '" (Acts 17:18, 32). The governor of Jerusalem, Felix, sent for Paul in order to hear his teaching. "And as he argued about justice and self-control and future judgment, Felix was alarmed and said: 'Go away for the present; when I have an opportunity I will summon you '" (Acts 24:25). Only the man who is humbly ready to repent knows God and obeys the gospel of the Lord Jesus. All unbelief consists in rejecting the gospel that "Jesus Christ is Lord" (Phil. 2:11). This gospel produces a crisis in the life of every man who hears it. It saves and judges.

The Eternal Punishment of the Godless (1:9)

⁹*They shall suffer the punishment of eternal destruction and exclusion from the presence of the Lord and from the glory of his might, . . .*

Paul describes the consequences of disobedience in the language the prophets used concerning the judgment. Eternal damnation consists in the non-fulfillment of the desire for eternal happiness, which is union with God. Eternal loneliness of the creature, cut off from the love of God revealed in Christ, will be experienced as the hardest punishment when Christ appears as the center of all life, of all men, and of the whole world.

Obedience to the gospel makes it possible to enter into the full life of the glory and power of God. The glory of God is the radiation of his power; it illuminates man, makes him happy and certain. A person who lives far from the glory of his power is threatened by anxiety and darkness. Paul is able to say to the Thessalonians, who are worried about their dead: " And so we shall always be with the Lord " (cf. 1 Thess. 4:13–18). Union with Christ is Paul's most fervent wish: " My desire is to depart and be with Christ " (Phil. 1:23).

The Glorification of the Lord at the End of Time (1: 10)

[10a] . . . *when he comes on that day to be glorified in his saints, and to be marveled at in all who have believed,* . . .

At the return of the Lord two events will take place: " on that day " he will punish the disobedient, and he will take up the faithful into his glory. The great event of the end of time will be for the former a catastrophe, for the latter radiant joy. " Blessed are you that weep now, for you shall laugh " (Lk. 6:21).

In power and glory the Lord will burst forth from his humble hiddenness. Then the true position of the Son of man will finally be revealed for all the world to see. He will appear with the saints and the faithful; they will form the guard of honor for the judge of the world. Like " his mighty angels " (1:7b), they will come with the Lord to the judgment.

The saving of those who have been obedient in faith takes place to the glory of God. When the faithful see the Lord " face to face " (1 Cor. 13:12), the great praise of God will begin. The songs of the redeemed will ring out: " We give thanks to thee, Lord God Almighty, who art and who wast, that thou hast taken thy great power and begun to reign " (Rev. 11:17). This day will bring the church to its perfect end.

The whole sentence shows us the longing of the early church

for the final fulfillment. It is as if Paul were saying: "On that day the whole of creation will celebrate the victory of God. Then God will be our all in all and that is our longing and our salvation." This longing for the approaching fulfillment must always be alive in the church.

[10b]. . . *because our testimony to you was believed.*

The description of the end as a fulfillment reminds Paul of the beginnings of the community. All the joy and glorification comes from the fact that the community had accepted the word of the Apostle as the word of God. His testimony had been accepted and led to faith. "We also thank God constantly for this, that when you received the word of God that you heard from us, you accepted it not as the word of man but as what it really is, the word of God, which is at work in you believers " (1 Thess. 2:13).

Intercession (1:11–12)

All believers await "that day." No man knows when the day and the hour of the mighty revelation of the Son of man will come. Thus all the faithful must wait patiently and endure. The main thing is to preserve the faith in all temptations and oppressions. Faith is always endangered. Only God, who is faithful to us, can complete the good work that he has begun in us; for we bear the treasure of the knowledge of the glory of God in earthen vessels (cf. 2 Cor. 4:7).

Intercessory prayer that the faith of the community may be preserved is an essential task of the pastor. That is why Paul, who has imparted to the Thessalonians the word of God, prays also that their faith may be preserved.

^{11a}*To this end we always pray for you, . . .*

Constant thanksgiving and intercession are the basic forms of apostolic prayer. " We give thanks to God always for you all, constantly mentioning you in our prayers " (1 Thess. 1 : 2). We are on our way, and fulfillment is still to come. The nearer the hour of God comes, the more dangerously and oppressively will Satan use his power. The powers and forces that poison the atmosphere are a constant threat to every believer and to the whole community. Thus the pastor lives in watchful concern for souls. His knowledge of the peril in which his flock stands makes him pray for them constantly.

^{11b}*. . . that our God may make you worthy of his call, . . .*

The community should show itself worthy of the great gift of grace of the call to become new men. The Christian must realize in his life that to which he is called. Although he is " not of this world," he can become unfaithful and again do the works of the flesh. In this case he would have received grace in vain. " Our God," however, can help us, so that we can live worthy of his call. Since God has revealed himself to us through Jesus Christ, Paul is able to say, full of pride : " The God and Father of our Lord Jesus Christ, the Father of mercies and God of all comfort " (2 Cor. 1 : 3). In the following intercession Paul shows how one becomes worthy of his call.

^{11c}*. . . and may fulfill every good resolve and work of faith by his power, . . .*

The new life that we have received is still imperfect. We have received a " pledge " of the glory to come. For as long as we live as pilgrims and strangers in this world we must always pray for the " fulfillment in power." It is a long path that leads to this fulfillment. Day by day the Christian must open himself more and more to God's work for him, so that he can grow ever more to the " human fulfillment of Christ." The sign of a maturing of the new life is a visible strengthening of basic Christian attitudes. Paul now tells us what the signs of growth are.

First, there is the joy in doing good. Paul is not speaking here of a natural morality. Before the coming of Christ both pagans in their immorality and the Jews in their complacent legalistic piety were lost. Only the believer can be saved. A man who has received the Holy Spirit and lives his life in faith and love is also able to realize in his life that which is pleasing to God. Thus all joy in doing good is a fruit of the Holy Spirit. " But the fruit of the Spirit is love, joy, peace, patience, kindness, goodness, faithfulness, gentleness, self-control " (Gal. 5 : 22).

The perfection of the work of faith is the goal that God wants to reach in his community. The individual believer and the whole community are to become more and more like Christ. In Paul also the Lord was at work. From his conversion to the moment when he was able to say : " It is no longer I who live, but Christ who lives in me " (Gal. 2 : 20), he had had to go through a maturing process. Mature faith is able to say : " Christ is my life " (Phil. 1 : 21). Now the only standard is the new knowledge of the supreme greatness of Christ : " For Jews demand signs and Greeks seek wisdom, but we preach Christ crucified, a stumbling block to Jews and folly to gentiles, but to those who are called, both Jews and Greeks, Christ the power of God and the wisdom of God. For the foolishness of God is wiser than men, and the

weakness of God is stronger than men " (1 Cor. 1:22–25).
" ' My grace is sufficient for you, for my power is made perfect
in weakness.' I will all the more gladly boast of my weakness,
that the power of Christ may rest upon me. For the sake of
Christ, then, I am content with weaknesses, insults, hardships,
persecutions, and calamities; for when I am weak, then I am
strong " (2 Cor. 12:9f.). God works in power. Invisible to
unbelievers, he, the unconquerable, is at work in this world.
He is completing his work. Men can be disobedient to his
gospel, they can be self-loving and proud, but God will set up
his dominion despite everything. Then every knee will bend
before his Son, to whom he hands over the dominion, and
everyone will testify, to the honor of the Father, " Jesus Christ
is Lord " (cf. Phil. 2:11).

Jesus warned the disobedient Pharisees. They had no cause
to boast proudly of their traditions, for God can make his power
effective in quite different ways. In the last times everyone—
Jews, gentiles, sinful and innocent alike—must submit to our
God, who has spoken his word to us in Christ. Otherwise, he
can cancel the election and choose other men who are more
grateful and more ready. " Bear fruits that befit repentance, and
do not begin to say to yourselves, ' We have Abraham as our
father '; for I tell you, God is able from these stones to raise up
children to Abraham " (Lk. 3:8).

*[12]. . . so that the name of our Lord Jesus may be glorified in
you, and you in him, according to the grace of our God and the
Lord Jesus Christ.*

The basic purpose of Paul's intercession is the glorification of
the Lord. Already in the Old Testament we find the connection

between the joy of the chosen and the glorification of Yahweh. Even the enemies of the faithful, those who hate them, know the connection between the joy of the chosen and the honor of God: " Let the Lord be glorified, that we may see your joy " (Is. 66:5).

Thus the glorification at the return of the Lord is a double-sided event. The elect will stand at the throne of the Lamb and in blissful joy sing to the Lord their new song: "And from the throne came a voice crying: ' Praise our God, all you his servants, you who fear him, small and great . . . let us rejoice and exalt and give him the glory, for the marriage of the Lamb has come ' " (Rev. 19:5, 7). Thus the ultimate goal of history is the final glorification of the Messiah, who will then be acknowledged as the head of mankind for ever and ever.

But the glory of the Lord of the world will also be the glory of the church. Whoever stands in the book of life, has confessed the Son of man on earth and glorified him, will then be able to become a citizen in the Holy City, the heavenly Jerusalem. All fear, care, and lamentation will then be taken from those who have glorified the Lord through their confession. " He will wipe away every tear from their eyes, and death shall be no more, neither shall there be mourning nor crying nor pain any more, for the former things have passed away. And he who sat upon the throne said: ' Behold, I make all things new ' " (Rev. 21:4f.). At the revelation of the Lord it will be seen that the praise and service of God are the ultimate fulfillment of the meaning of human life.

The basis of the glorification of the church is the grace of God. God shows to each generation anew his goodwill: " And his mercy is on those who fear him from generation to generation " (Lk. 1:50).

But in the last times the grace of God has become visible; it has taken form in " our Lord Jesus Christ." With great joy Paul proclaims to his community this new reality. " For it is God who said: ' Let light shine out of darkness,' who has shone in our hearts to give the light of the knowledge of the glory of God in the face of Christ " (2 Cor. 4:6).

THE MAIN CONCERNS OF THE LETTER
(2:1—3:16)

Warning Against an Error About the Return of Christ
(2:1–12)

An Urgent Request (2:1–2)

²:¹*Now concerning the coming of our Lord Jesus Christ and our
assembling to meet him, we beg you, brethren, *²ᵃ*not to be
quickly shaken in mind or excited, . . .*

Now the main part of the letter begins. Abuses that had appeared
in the community were the reason for Paul's writing the letter.
He does not want to take up these questions as a judge or as
the leader of the community, but as a brother among brothers.
This is why he asks the brethren to reject the false ideas. Paul
would like the community to make a free decision which comes
from a whole-hearted agreement. In the same spirit he writes
to Philemon: "I preferred to do nothing without your consent
in order that your goodness might not be by compulsion but
out of your own free will" (Philem. 14). While it is in any
way possible, Paul tries to deal with difficulties in love and
trust. The pastor and the servant of the word puts away all
personal and natural feelings. He is not concerned with counter-
ing a personal insult or calumny; he would rather preserve the
community in the truth and love of Christ.

Circumstances of which we have no further details led the church in Thessalonica to an enthusiastic immediate expectation of the return of the Lord. Their sobriety and vigilance, the basic attitudes of the Christian in the world, are endangered. The community which is watching for the Lord will one day form part of the triumphant procession of the returning Christ. All who have persevered in obedience and love will gather with the Lord and then take part in the great procession of victory at the end of time. As in public life kings and emperors are conducted solemnly into the town at their arrival, so the Lord also will move into the new city with his retinue and guard of honor. On that day the fervently awaited union of the church with Christ will take place. The Thessalonians had often seen the splendor and glory of the arrival of a king. There was happiness and rejoicing.

There is a rumor that the day of the Lord has arrived. This news has frightened many. There is great excitement, and no one listens any longer to calm and reasonable words. A wild ecstatic joy has broken out in the community as a result of this psychological stimulation. Probably, the abuses that Paul criticizes in 3:6-16 are also connected with this state of affairs. Many people no longer did any work and let themselves be supported by the community. They considered that it was not worth working, since the Lord could come any day.

In this situation Paul had to give an urgent warning. The condition into which the community has fallen is very dangerous. Even if the Christian has a burning longing for the day of the Lord and a profound desire for union with Christ, he must not lose his sobriety. The course of salvation history is ordered by God, so the warning of the Lord is always valid: " Watch therefore—for you will not know when the master of the house will come, in the evening or at midnight, or at cockcrow, or in the morning—lest he comes suddenly and finds you asleep" (Mk. 13:35f.). But what was the origin of this mood in the community?

²ᵇ. . . *either by spirit [of a prophet] or by word, or by letter purporting to be from us, to the effect that the day of the Lord has come.*

Obviously, Paul is not informed of the details of the background and origin of the rumors and excitements. There might be three reasons for them. A false prophet might have appeared who said that he had received the Spirit of God to tell the community that the day of the Lord had come. But it could also be pure rumor. A member of the community may have misinterpreted some statement of the apostolic tradition, perhaps in order to make himself interesting. Men try constantly to determine by calculation and reflection the date of the return of the Lord. The Christian should not let himself be confused by these over-clever people. It is a popular method of false teachers and " false brethren " (cf. 2 Cor. 11:26) to put their thoughts and ideas in the mouths of attested authorities of the church. This makes them appear worthy of belief and confidence among the community. People then think that it must be true, if Paul has said it. But Paul is not interested in the origin of the rumor, but in the error itself. He must discover and repudiate it and all its consequences.

A Reminder About the Coming of the Anti-Christ (2:3–5)

Man has a profound impatience for perfection. He wants to have security and finality. Thus he presses towards the end of history.

He wants to make God bring the end soon. Fanatics appear and announce that the day of the Lord has arrived! Paul replies to these people with a firm " No." These enthusiasts in Thessalonica fail to see that before the return of the Lord a number of other events will take place. His return will be accompanied by signs and events, as to whose nature we have only hints. Paul wants to direct the community's attention firmly to the fact that God has willed that there be an intermediate period. Between the present and the return of the Lord there is a period of time that one must pass through soberly and watchfully. In this one is helped by a faith that is able to read the signs of the time correctly and calmly.

[3a]*Let no one deceive you in any way; . . .*

The Christian is endangered by many errors. He must tread the right path of truth and love. But in the world lies and egoism are constantly exalted into teaching. Vigilance is necessary in order not to fall victim to the intrigues of the enemies of Christ. No one in the community is to be able to spread abroad a false teaching about the return of the Lord.

[3b]. . . *for that day will not come, unless the rebellion comes first, and the man of lawlessness is revealed, the son of perdition,* [4]*who opposes and exalts himself against every so-called god or object of worship, so that he takes his seat in the temple of God, proclaiming himself to be God.*

In the last time of all, great affliction will come upon the world. Suffering, hate, and destruction will overwhelm men, because love will have grown cold in many hearts. This affliction will also be a great temptation for believers. The saints will be able to withstand it only because the Lord shortens this period of temptation. Many Christians will depart from the teaching they have received and from the new life and return again to error and sin. They will renounce the conversion to God that they had made in the obedience of faith and leave the community of Christ. Turning away is the opposite of conversion, as Paul describes it in the First Epistle to the Thessalonians: ". . . how you turned to God from idols, to serve a living and true God, and to wait for his Son from heaven, whom he raised from the dead, Jesus who delivers us from the wrath to come " (1 Thess. 1:9f.). A man who lets himself be carried away by joy at the thought that the Lord can return at any moment knows nothing of the dangerous and unhappy situation that mankind must go through at the end of time.

It is the appearance of the anti-Christ that will make men fall away. The powers and forces of the anti-Christ have already been at work in history and have moved men to fall away, to betray, to lie, and to murder. But in the last times the anti-Christ himself will appear and reveal his satanic power.

Paul describes the manner of the anti-Christ with words from the Old Testament. The prophet Daniel had foretold the man of lawlessness: " He shall speak words against the Most High, and shall wear out the saints of the Most High, and shall think to change the times and the law " (Dan. 7:25). The figure of destruction of the last times contradicts radically the holy will of God. The arrogant " No " of human pride will take shape in the man of lawlessness. This negation of the will of God means ruin for man. Man has separated himself from God through his own will. Whoever denies the will of God and speaks a conscious and clear " No " to him falls victim to destruction. The purpose and activity of the anti-Christ is directed towards opposing God's holy order in creation. But since this disorder cannot remain, he will finally be overcome.

Paul gives a picture of the anti-Christ by describing the things he does. Again he uses an image that the prophet Daniel had used of the godless king: " The king shall do according to his will; he shall exalt himself and magnify himself above every god " (Dan. 11 : 16). The sin of the anti-Christ consists in two attitudes which mean the ruin of any creature: opposition to the order of God and self-pride. Thus the nature of the opponent of God resides in his boundless glorification of self.

The proud and arrogant attitude of the anti-Christ emerges in his deeds that are directed against God. He seeks to cast him down from his eternal throne and make himself God. In the Old Testament the prophet Ezekiel was forced to speak to the proud Prince of Tyre the word of the Lord: " Because your heart is proud, and you have said, ' I am a god, I sit in the seat of the gods, in the heart of the seas,' yet you are but a man, and no God, though you consider yourself as wise as a God " (Ezek. 28 : 2). Where men honor the eternal and holy God, the son of destruction takes his place. Here he will receive the worship and acknowledgment of men. False imagining, pride, and self-complacency are the characteristics of the man of lawlessness and the son of destruction. God is to be supplanted for ever.

⁵Do you not remember that when I was still with you I told you this?

The community should really know these things. In his missionary preaching Paul had proclaimed to them the true teaching about the last times. He had already said then that the anti-

Christ would come and that Christians had to wait in patience and vigilance for the Lord. He was concerned in his preaching to point out that no man knows the hour when the Lord will come. In his first letter to the community he wrote quite clearly: " But as to the times and the seasons, brethren, you have no need to have anything written to you. For you yourselves know well that the day of the Lord will come like a thief in the night " (1 Thess. 5:1–3). But now, despite this, he must chide the community for its false ideas, although he was able only shortly before to offer it as a model for the whole of Macedonia and Achaia.

Necessary Additional Teaching (2:6–12)

The Full Revelation of the Anti-Christ
Is Still to Come (2:6–7)

⁶And you know what is restraining him now so that he may be revealed in his time. ⁷For the mystery of lawlessness is already at work; only he who now restrains it will do so until he is out of the way.

The basic ideas of Paul's missionary preaching are now clear again in the memory of the community. Thus Paul is able to point out particular elements of his teaching that must still be familiar to them, but he does not go through them again. So we do not know what restrains the anti-Christ at the moment from revealing himself finally. Hence the appearance of the anti-Christ will not take place in the present, but in the future, because in the present there is still something that prevents him from appearing.

Despite his glorification of self the anti-Christ must obey God. The revelation of the anti-Christ has its place in the course of salvation history. God alone, in his power, determines the whole course of the history of the world. Even his opponents ultimately are at his disposal. Thus the Christian can live patiently in the moment and understand directly what it asks of him. He must not fail to grasp the moment because of fantastic ideas concerning his expectation of the future. Every believer must humbly accept his place in the course of history that God has willed.

The personal appearance of the anti-Christ is still to come, although his destructive powers are already at work among us. The murderer of men from the beginning, the father of lies poisons the atmosphere in which men live. He wants to make them fall away from God. Thus the mystery of lawlessness is already at work now, leading men to fall away.

Since the coming of Christ every period of the church's history is the " last time." The gospel is proclaimed everywhere; men receive the word of truth and are converted. But after this they often fall away again, dissolving their relation with God. In the parable of the seed the Lord says that the word will bring a hundredfold fruit; but much good seed of the word of God will be wasted because men do not wholly accept the word and therefore come to grief in their difficulties (Mk. 4 : 13ff.).

In the last times two things always happen : the proclamation of the gospel and the acceptance of the " law of freedom " (Jas. 2 : 12). " The gospel must first be preached to all nations " (Mk. 13 : 10). But then there is also falling away. " Now the Spirit expressly says that in later times some will depart from the faith by giving heed to deceitful spirits and doctrines of demons " (1 Tim. 4 : 1).

Both obedience in faith and opposition to it are part of this world that is passing away. In every form of self-complacency and self-glorification in a man the present activity of the anti-Christ is made manifest. At the end of time he will show himself openly, until the Lord makes him powerless at his own appearance. Paul has already pointed out (2:6) that the anti-Christ is still hindered by his opponent from using his full destructive force and his direct influence. The Evil One is held in check until the hour that God has set him has come. We do not know anything further about this opponent of the anti-Christ, only that there is a being that restrains the anti-Christ from exercising his full power immediately and for ever. At the end of time he who holds back the son of perdition is removed, perhaps by force. Then the conflict between God and his opponent will reach its most intense state. A struggle will begin which demands from every man an ultimate decision. Thus the life of a Christian must be a constant training in commitment to the will of God, so that in the struggle with the powers and forces of evil he is able to remain on the side of God.

The Final Appearance and Destruction of the Anti-Christ (2:8)

[8]*And then the lawless one will be revealed, and the Lord Jesus will slay him with the breath of his mouth and destroy him by his appearing and his coming.*

At the last time the lawless one will be able to show himself because his opponent has been removed. Paul says quite firmly: ". . . and then the lawless one will be revealed." This is the beginning of the end. He will perform his powerful deeds in all openness. He will be impressive, and no one able to resist him. Then he will no longer work in secret against God to the injury of men, but he will be able to proclaim his enmity to God quite openly and use every means to force men to bend the knee to him. But all this will be only a deceitful pose, since he only appears to possess full power. The lawless one who opposes God with his whole being will be conquered at the appearance of the Lord. The great period in which he feels like God will end miserably. It is true that he will perform mighty wonders and signs, as Paul goes on to show, but the Lord will easily overcome him.

Paul uses the words of the prophet Isaiah to show what will happen at his coming. " He shall smite the earth with the rod of his mouth, and with the breath of his lips he shall slay the wicked " (Is. 11:4). Paul depicts the coming of the Lord in sharp colors. His very coming will convict the lawless one. God reveals himself, and through this unbelief is judged. When God, the Lord of life and the world, visibly appears before all men, there is no longer any discussion and any resistance. Then the power of evil is at an end.

The stronger one, our Lord Jesus, will put an end to the power of egoism and disobedience. As a pastor, Paul wants above all to give comfort: it is true that the anti-Christ will appear, but his destructive dominion will come to an end. This happens because the power of Satan has been broken long ago and he is only carrying out on the earth a last desperate fight. The Lord himself saw this: " I saw Satan fall like lightning from heaven " (Lk. 10:18). There is no struggle between the powers. The anti-Christ is annihilated by a command of the Lord. The word of God will prove itself as irresistibly powerful.

At his return the Lord will show himself in glory. He will be visible in light. The light is the reflection of his radiant power. The holiness and glory of God will appear. " His face was like the sun shining in full strength " (Rev. 1 : 16). Thus the Lord in his power is able to disarm the anti-Christ and destroy him. Nothing more will remain of evil, and the faithful will find peace with God.

THE CONSEQUENCES FOR NON-BELIEVERS (2 :9–12)

⁹The coming of the lawless one by the activity of Satan will be with all power and with pretended signs and wonders, ¹⁰and with all wicked deception for those who are to perish, because they refused to love the truth and so be saved.

The victory of the Lord is assured. He will triumph over the opponent of God who brings ruin. But the faithful, whose salvation is not finally assured in the present time, must be prepared for the destructive working of Satan. The lawless one will come. Just as Christ will one day appear in might and power and all will have to bend the knee before him, so there will also be a mighty coming of the anti-Christ. This will take place in great power, for behind him stands Satan. Generally, the New Testament speaks only of the glorious coming of Jesus Christ as the transfigured one at the judgment. But here Paul balances the mighty coming of the Lord with the apparently mighty " coming " of the lawless one. The son of perdition will appear in the power and deceptive glory of Satan.

The anti-Christ will also work powerful deeds, which will impress men. A rejection of him or a critical attitude towards

SECOND EPISTLE TO THE THESSALONIANS 131

him will be unintelligible to everyone. The seer John has described for us the powerful coming of the anti-Christ: " It [the beast from the earth] works great signs, even making fire come down from heaven to earth in the sight of men: and by the signs which it is allowed to work in the presence of the beast, it deceives those who dwell on earth " (Rev. 13:13f.).

Signs and pretended wonders will show that the anti-Christ has power. The miracles of Christ are also signs. They show the redemptive power of God, made manifest in the liberating work of Jesus. Healing the sick and raising the dead point to the bliss and joy that is to come. Thus the miracles show concretely what the Lord is proclaiming to men. The miracles of Jesus often result in the eye-witnesses receiving faith. The pretended wonders and signs of the anti-Christ are especially dangerous because they too point to a power which can be followed. But if a man trusts these miracles, he falls victim to a false power which collapses at the decisive moment and brings ruin to him. A Christian has to be very objective. He must be able to differentiate between the signs of God and the pretended wonders of Satan. If a man trusts these powerful deeds of Satan, he will learn at the judgment that he is on the wrong side.

By his seductions Satan will gain respect and deceive men. All the proofs of Satan's power, his false wonders and signs, have only one purpose: they seek to lead men to wickedness. But wickedness is opposition to the will of God. Through his power Satan will bring about a rebellion of men against God. Then the church of God will need " the endurance and faith of the saints " (Rev. 13:10).

The appearance of Christ and the proclamation of his message cause a division among men. It is impossible to ignore it; it can lead men only either to life or to death. Thus there are men who are saved and men who are lost. It is the perilous and weighty time of decision. The salvation of every man depends ultimately on his attitude towards Christ crucified and risen. The gospel of the despised and ridiculed Lord on the cross is for many proud spirits a folly that is not worth talking about. Complacent and self-assured, they reject this gospel of poverty and obedience. But this is their ruin. " For the word of the cross is folly to those who are perishing, but to us who are being saved it is the power of God. For it is written, ' I will destroy the wisdom of the wise, and the cleverness of the clever I will thwart ' " (1 Cor. 1 : 18f.).

The man who declares himself the measure of all things is no longer open to God's message of salvation. The father of lies and the murderer of men from the beginning, as scripture calls Satan, causes men to be proud. In his pride he no longer listens to the message of salvation. The apostles are under the dominion of God and must proclaim the dominion of God; they are messengers of God who provoke a decision and hence a division in man : " For we are the aroma of Christ to God among those who are being saved and among those who are perishing, to one a fragrance from death to death, to the other a fragrance from life to life " (2 Cor. 2 : 15f.). The portion of the proud will be death. By rejecting the message of salvation in this world, they have rejected living communion with God through Christ, the only true life.

The reality of the healing love of God comes to us in the truth of the gospel. Love of truth is love of the good news. It is the message of Christ, the Lord and the Son of God, who can say of himself: " I am the way, the truth, and the life " (Jn. 14 : 6). The truth is realized as " the word of life " (Phil. 2 : 16) in love. On this basis Paul sees how Christians must fight against false teachings: "We may no longer be children, tossed to and fro and carried about with every wind of doctrine, by the cunning of men, by their craftiness in deceitful wiles. Rather, speaking the truth in love, we are to grow up in every way into him who is the head, into Christ" (Eph. 4:14f.). Love of truth is openness and readiness for the gospel. The man who consciously withdraws from the truth of God, robs his life of its real meaning.

The acceptance of truth always takes place in obedience and humility. It is the attitude of the poor and of children. In his preaching Christ declared that the poor and the children were blessed. We are called to bring about in ourselves this basic attitude so that we may be saved.

[11]*Therefore God sends upon them a strong delusion, to make them believe what is false,* [12]*so that all may be condemned who did not believe the truth but had pleasure in unrighteousness.*

The proclamation of the gospel has its reverse side. In the word of God there is a powerful force that transforms the world, but it also calls for counter-forces. A man who resists the power of the word succumbs to the great pull of the energy of the anti-Christ. Whoever rejects the truth is swept into the whirlpool of seduction, which pulls down everything and destroys it. If someone falls victim to seduction his life disintegrates, and he is in danger of death. In the last times one must not treat one's life lightly. "Look carefully then how you walk, not as unwise men but as wise, making the most of the time, because the days are evil" (Eph. 5:15f.). God himself gives seduction its power, because a man who in a time of crisis does not decide for the truth is already judged.

Whoever abandons himself to seduction to evil, appearing and working in the name of the Messiah, is in the world like a ship without a compass on the high seas. He drifts through this world and must have an open ear for the saving teaching which evil purports to provide. But the life of man can be healed only by the communion with God the creator that is offered and made possible by Christ. It is this high good that is ultimately rejected in unbelief and disobedience. In the light of God a lie is what is opposed to the truth of God: " Who is the liar but he who denies that Jesus is the Christ? This is the anti-Christ, he who denies the Father and the Son. No one who denies the Son has the Father " (1 Jn. 2:22f.). Paul shows the impossible contradiction in which those who have let themselves be seduced are involved: they think they have found God and serve him, but in reality they are believing in a lie. In full conviction they are following a false teaching and submit blindly to their self-made " dogma."

God takes the disobedience of man seriously. To reject the offer of God's love, which has come to us through his Son, is to condemn oneself. The self-willed disobedience of man is its own punishment. We are already at the beginning of the new world. The judgment has already come. Here and now the living God holds judgment. The consequence of unrighteousness and the rejection of the truth that is realized in love is already judgment. " Truly, truly, I say to you, he who hears my word and believes him who sent me, has eternal life; he does not come into judgment; but has passed from death to life " (Jn. 5:24). " He who believes in him is not condemned; he who does not believe is condemned already, because he has not believed in the name of the only Son of God " (Jn. 3:,18).

Finally, Paul contrasts the two basic attitudes that are possible after the appearance of Christ: belief in the truth and joy in unrighteousness. Humble openness to the truth and the love of God ensures for man salvation and with it the goods of the last times: peace, freedom, joy, and happiness. The proud and complacent rejection of God's offer of salvation becomes judgment for the unrighteous. His attitude finally becomes fixed. He will have to live without God, that is in eternal dissatisfaction because of his wrong decision, and in eternal frustration, without joy and hope. In these words we sense something of the stern and powerful God who is not mocked. The prophet Jeremiah proclaimed in strong language the greatness and power of the judging God: " There is none like thee, O Lord; thou art great, and thy name is great in might. Who would not fear thee, O King of the nations? For this is thy due; for among all the wise ones of the nations and in all their kingdoms there is none like thee. They are both stupid and foolish; the instruction of idols is but wood . . . But the Lord is the true God; he is the living God and the everlasting king. At his wrath the earth quakes, and the nations cannot endure his indignation " (Jer. 10:6-10).

The Right Spirit of Faith (2:13—3:5)

Thanksgiving for the Election of the Brethren (2:13-14)

[13]*But we are bound to give thanks to God always for you, brethren beloved by the Lord, because God chose you from the beginning to be saved, through sanctification by the Spirit and belief in the truth.*

After the very serious account of the judgment of God on men who let themselves be seduced by evil, Paul gives joyful thanks.

Thanksgiving for election is always stronger and deeper when seen against the somber background of possible damnation and condemnation. The fate of disobedience and the divine punishment make even clearer the greatness of the call of the church. The salvation of all the brethren and sisters is the happy reason for the joyful thanksgiving of Paul. He uses the same words of thanksgiving as at the beginning of the letter, but after what he has said he is able to give a deeper reason why it was right and proper to give thanks. Our debt of gratitude is so urgent because of the divine grace which is imparted to us without our deserving it.

Our election by the grace of God is expressed even in the impressive mode of address that Paul uses here. In it he states with emotion the actual situation that exists: " Brethren beloved by the Lord." The Lord has given us his love. All who belong to the community have accepted this offer of love with humility and obedience and through this have been justified in Christ. In this way brotherhood comes into being. All who have submitted to the yardstick and the will of God belong together and come together. The love of God is the bond that unites all the members of the church and makes them become the family of God.

God has given to the church in Thessalonica a particular sign of his grace. It was here that the gospel of salvation was proclaimed and accepted for the first time in the province of Macedonia. A community was formed that was exemplary in its new life and a model for the church through the whole world (1 Thess. 1:8). The Lord wants everyone to be saved. But he works in history. He carries out his saving work through particular calls and promptings. Thus the call and the grace of God come to many men and many communities in a quite special way. They are chosen for a particular service of witness or love. This always happens for the whole church. Particular calls are a gift and a commission for an individual or for the community. The community of Thessalonica was to be a power center of the word. " For not only has the word of the Lord sounded forth from you in Macedonia and Achaia, but your faith in God has gone forth everywhere, so that we need not say anything " (1 Thess. 1 : 8).

It is necessary to be reminded of the event of conversion, since the forces of God are constantly at work. Only someone who knows about God's work in the church can constantly open himself afresh to this activity. In a very brief form Paul presents the basic elements of conversion. He is able to assume knowledge of them in this community and thus restricts himself to a short reminder.

Fundamental to every conversion is the fact that God reveals himself to man. Man can then have a share in the life of God. Through this man who had become, through error and sin, the " possession " of the prince of this world, again becomes possession of his creator. He is a new creation, a new man who can sing to the Lord in a new garment the new song of the redeemed. This is the sanctification by the Spirit. In other letters Paul described this process in detail: " We were buried, therefore, with him by baptism into death, so that as Christ was raised from the dead by the glory of the Father, we too might walk in newness of life " (Rom. 6:4). " If anyone is in Christ, he is a new creation; the old has passed away, behold, the new has come. All this is from God, who through Christ reconciled us to himself and gave us the ministry of reconciliation " (2 Cor. 5 : 17f.).

God's saving work is bound in our time to the Lord Jesus. His name is invoked at baptism, he is at work in all the actions of the church and refashions man. The response to sanctification by the Spirit is belief in truth. The new man, who has crucified the old man with his passions and desires (Gal. 5:24), can rely lovingly on the activity of God. In his new life he learns with joy through God's work the truth of the promise of the Lord: " He who does what is true comes to the light " (Jn. 3:21). Ever more and unreservedly he gives himself over to the word of the gospel. The heart is freed and purified of all selfishness and all pride, so that God can fill the heart of the new man through Christ and take up his dwelling in him.

[14]To this he called you through our gospel, so that you may obtain the glory of our Lord Jesus Christ.

In the fullness of time God sent his Son. He has spoken to men. He gave his apostles the task of spreading the word of truth. " He who hears you hears me " (Lk. 10:16). In fulfilling this commission the Apostle has not only the right but the duty to point out that his word is binding. The gospel of Christ lives in the church through the preaching of the apostles and seeks to reach all men. The preaching of the good news makes us hear the voice of God. Against the words of men stands the eternal and binding word of God that must be accepted in faith. " And we also thank God constantly for this, that when you received the word of God which you heard from us, you accepted it not as the word of man but as what it really is, the word of God, which is at work in you believers " (1 Thess. 2:13).

By accepting the " word of life " man receives salvation. The goal is the acquisition of the glory of our Lord Jesus Christ. The Apostle would far rather die and already be wholly with Christ in eternal perfection. His whole longing is for final union with Christ. Thus he speaks, constantly, with yearning and enthusiasm, of community in and with Christ. With the death and resurrection of the Lord this act of God's grace has appeared. Christ, the humiliated man, persecuted and killed by his oppressors, has been taken into the glory of the Father. He has received his might and his power, and is now the head and the fulfillment of the world. We are moving towards this fulfillment.

These are important words of comfort for the church in Thessalonica. It is going through a period of suffering and must tread the dark way of the passion of the Lord in his footsteps. The path of a man who follows Christ is determined by a mysterious law that is very difficult for human beings to understand. The risen Lord had to tell the disciples on the road to Emmaus, who were going home perplexed and unhappy, of this way of the Messiah: " O foolish men, and slow of heart to believe all that the prophets have spoken! Was it not necessary that the Christ should suffer these things and enter into his glory?" (Lk. 24:25f.).

Exhortation to Steadfastness (2:15–17)

[15]So then, brethren, stand firm and hold to the traditions which you were taught by us, either by word of mouth or by letter.

Judgment and glorification—these are the two possibilities for every man at the end of time. No man is sure of salvation while he is on the way of pilgrimage. In an age of rebellion, unrest, and false doctrines the Christian is always in danger. As Paul sadly sees, it is possible also to receive grace in vain. The preservation of a new life in us and in our brethren is our responsibility. No one must neglect the great offer of God's salvation or give it second place in his life. Everyone should awaken to and increase the sense of responsibility for his faith. The Christian must stand firmly and, in the face of all the struggles, oppressions and seductions of the world and the son of perdition, remain true to his position. The brethren must always expect struggles in this world, in which one has to prove one's steadfastness. " Only let your manner of life be worthy of the gospel of Christ, so that whether I come and see you or am absent, I may hear of you that you stand firm in one spirit, with one mind striving side by side for the faith of the gospel, and not frightened in anything by your opponents. This is a clear omen to them of their destruction, but of your salvation, and that from God " (Phil. 1 : 27ff.).

Paul now describes in some detail what he means by Christian steadfastness. Love of truth is shown in fidelity to the tradition that the community has received from him. The truth that is handed down is not a human word, not the private opinion of an apostle, it is the word of God. But the word of God that is handed down to us is not at our disposal, in the sense that we can subtract from it or add to it. The community must submit to the word in obedience. Then it is remaining true to the gospel of Christ. " Now I would remind you, brethren, in what terms I preached to you the gospel, which you received, in which you stand, by which you are saved, if you hold it fast—unless you believed in vain " (1 Cor. 15 : 1ff.). As the missionary of Christ, Paul himself is wholly committed to tradition : " For I delivered it to you as of first importance what I also received . . ." (1 Cor. 15 : 3).

Apostolic instruction in the tradition takes place in two ways :

in preaching and in pastoral letters. Paul came to the town and preached the new gospel there for the first time. Men came to faith, and thus the churches came into being. Through his letters Paul had to continue to instruct the newly-founded communities in the faith, and counter possible errors or abuses if he himself or one of his helpers was not able to come to the community. To these forms of pastoral letters we owe the writings of the New Testament. They are the handing down of the gospel of God's salvation in Jesus Christ in the shape of " scripture."

[16]*Now may our Lord Jesus Christ himself, and God our Father, who loved us and gave us eternal comfort and good hope through grace,* [17]*comfort your hearts and establish them in every good work and word.*

But the preaching of the gospel of salvation is not an impersonal communication. It takes place always in a personal commitment. Thus the message of salvation that the scriptural writers give to us bears the marks of their personal characteristics. It is a wholly personal commitment to the word of God that they are handing on. Paul's writings are confessional writings. His exemplary way of life makes the good news credible. The pastor Paul adds to his exhortation to fidelity a prayer for the community. God himself must support this intention and the readiness of the church with his power. A helper of the Lord must constantly remember the communities in his prayers so that the work begun can also be finished.

Paul presents his intercession in a solemn form. Probably he is using here a form of speech that is customary in the liturgical worship of the early church. The communities prayed for one another in this way. In this prayer Jesus Christ comes at the beginning of the intercession. Paul seeks to point out here the order of salvation. Only through Christ does the Christian come to the Father. We receive love, comfort, and hope from the Father, but always only through Jesus Christ. Thus he stands between us men and the Father, as mediator and saviour. Here, in one of the earliest letters of the New Testament, Paul declares the divinity of Christ. For him it was never in doubt that the Son of God had come into the world and thus was truly able to give to men life and salvation.

The basis of our salvation is the love of the Father. In all their sufferings the community is to experience this love. We received it at our election, but again and again after that through the guidance of God's grace. The love of God also reveals itself in the fact that he opens himself to sinners and shows them a meaningful new way of life. A sign of genuine love is the readiness to do everything for the beloved. God has " proved " his love in his Son, who gave his life for his friends. In this love of God men can breathe freely and be joyful.

The love of God reveals itself in comfort and hope. Through the truth itself that is handed down we receive the power to endure in our situation. " For whatever was written in former days was written for our instruction, that by steadfastness and by the encouragement of the scriptures we might have hope " (Rom. 15:4). The Christian receives constant comfort by looking up to God, who grants him his love. Thus his whole life acquires meaning. All the questions that beset him receive an answer from God. If a man listens to the word that is handed down, he becomes, as it were, clairvoyant, understands his own age, and knows about the future. He remains in the present situation, with all its difficulties. For him everything is only a passage to the final union with Christ. Everything receives its meaning from the fact that one day we will be gathered with Christ. Thus the " God of all comfort " (2 Cor. 1 : 3) gives man the only genuine comfort.

The Christian is comforted by looking towards the future. Everything will work out well. We already have now a pledge of the coming glory in the grace and love of God; but eventually we will be taken up into his radiant glory. This vision of the future is the hope of the Christian, which gives him joy now.

In comfort and hope the hearts of the faithful are strengthened. There is now no need for them to despair. Perhaps many men will not understand this life. His joy cannot be taken from the believer, even if his life in the view of the men who measure it by the yardsticks of this world is a difficult one. Paul was a model for his community in this fundamental joy. " I am filled with comfort. With all our affliction, I am overjoyed " (2 Cor. 7 : 4).

In this strength and joy that come from the Lord, the Christian is able to fulfill his commandment: " Love one another; even as I have loved you " (Jn. 13 : 34). This attitude is shown in good works and good words. The Christian life is not realized in enforced exertions of the will. Love in word and deed is rather the overflow of a heart that is full of comfort, hope, and joy. Thus Paul prays first for the foundation of a solid faith, and only then for the right attitude in word and work.

A Request for Intercession (3 :1–2)

3:1*Finally, brethren, pray for us that the word of the Lord may speed on and triumph, as it did among you, *2and that we may be delivered from wicked and evil men; for not all have faith.*

Paul tells the community the two things for which he desires their prayers. The main thing is the proclamation of the word. May the word speed on unhindered! The word of God is not bound or dependent on those who preach it. But the servants of the word are dependent on the prayer of the community. In prayer the community opens itself in confidence to the Lord who is guiding his church. Paul wants to feel that he is supported in his service by the prayer of the church.

The prayer of the Apostle for his community must be followed by the prayer of the community for the Apostle. The church is a brotherhood in which everyone has to help everyone else. It is not to be a community that needs looking after, led by someone who is particularly suited to the task. Every brother must also be concerned for the work of the apostles. Prayer for the servants of the word should never be lacking in the community. Without the prayer of the church even the word of the Apostle runs the danger of becoming merely a human word, and therefore without effect. The apostles do not proclaim the word in their own right. Rather, they are " God's servants in the gospel of Christ " (1 Thess. 3:2).

Paul makes a curious sounding request: that the word of the Lord may speed on. Is the word something that is independent of the apostles? In the preaching of the apostles it is Jesus Christ who is speaking. But he is the Lord who cannot be conquered. Those who proclaim the word of God can be persecuted and put in chains, but the word of God still spreads with great power. Paul can testify to this while in prison: ". . . the gospel for which I am suffering and wearing fetters like a criminal. But the word of God is not fettered " (2 Tim. 2:9). The mission still has great tasks to perform. Paul sees the whole of Europe before him. The word is to speed on everywhere. He and his helpers have received this commission from the Lord. All the churches must share in the missionary zeal of the apostles by praying for those who proclaim the word.

The word of God that spreads over the whole earth like a fire finds men everywhere and compels them to make a decision. Now that they have heard of Christ they must decide. Everywhere in the world the word of God forces men into a crisis. If men accept it, they submit in obedience. They experience its vitalizing and purifying power. Redeemed and liberated from the darkness in which they were once compelled to live, they break out into a song of praise of the word of God. Thus the word of God is praised and glorified. This glorification is always also a confession of faith: Your word is truth, light, and life, O Lord, we believe you!

In Thessalonica the glorification of the word of God took place in an exemplary way. The Christians turned away from idols to the living God. They had the joyful experience of conversion. In this joy they praised the word of God. Now Paul is asking for their intercession. The community which has accepted and experienced the healing powers of the word of God is now to pray that in the other towns to which Paul is going people might be equally open and prepared for the word. If a man is redeemed and liberated by the word, he must pray for all his human brothers that they also may receive the light of the gospel. Faith must not be simply a possession that one holds on to but must urge one, in the most different ways, to communicate it. Intercessory prayer on behalf of man is a way of helping the proclamation of the word. Since the word produces a crisis in a man and calls him to repentance and obedience, it annoys evil men who do not want to give up their pride and their sin. The apostles are exposed to constant dangers from all sides. Paul had had to undergo many persecutions and hurtful treatment by

Jews and gentiles. He was firmly and clearly proclaiming salvation in Jesus Christ. This aroused the opposition of the " enemies of the cross." It was especially painful to him that the Jews, his " kinsmen by race " (Rom. 9:3), continually persecuted him. He had often seen that the gentiles listened readily to the gospel, but the Jews provoked the people and the authorities against him by attributing dishonest motives to him. He had found that to be particularly the case in Thessalonica.

The greatest missionary of the church saw, with sober realism, that a complete conversion of the world is not possible. The word of God comes up against resistance in men who refuse to open themselves to it. Faith is not for everybody. Men are divided by the word of God. The preaching of the apostles cannot, nor does it desire to, put pressure on those who hear it. A decision for faith must always take place in the greatest possible freedom. It is in the innermost part of his being that man says " Yes " to God and to his saving work. Love cannot be commanded. It can only be accepted or rejected. The preaching of an apostle is always a wooing in love of every individual man who is to open himself to the love of God and make the right response to it. Paul had often experienced this division of men: " He expounded the matter to them from morning till evening, testifying to the kingdom of God, and trying to convince them about Jesus both from the law of Moses and from the prophets. And some were convinced by what he said, while others disbelieved " (Acts 28:23f.).

Renewed Strengthening in Faith (3:3–5)

³*But the Lord is faithful; he will strengthen you and guard you from evil.*

Men are often unfaithful. They do not preserve their relationship with God and turn away again from their creator. Even if faith is not for everybody and many do not acquire it, the Christian still has no cause for alarm. For the Lord is faithful. He does not begin something and then lose interest and put it aside. When men are ready for the Lord and remain so, he will give them his strong hand so that they will be able to continue to follow him despite all their weakness. " And I ensure that he who began a good work in you will bring it to completion at the day of Christ " (Phil. 1 : 6). Our Christian life is something that is constantly threatened. We are always in danger of succumbing. For Christians who live out their faith in the world consciously and faithfully, the faithfulness of God is the sure foundation on which they are able to stand. But Paul's anxious warning is intended for them also: " Let any one who thinks that he stands take heed lest he fall " (1 Cor. 10 : 12).

Sinners are to know that God does not desire the death of a sinner, but that he should live. If a man does not let go of the hand of God, even in guilt and sin, and asks for pardon, he is forgiven. God will not withhold from any man the gift of faith if he prepares himself for the message of salvation. The faithfulness of God is shown in this also. But he does not force himself on any man against his own decision. We can understand more and more why Paul can thank the Lord so fervently for the strength of the brethren's faith.

The Evil One seeks to destroy the work of God. But God steps as a " guardian " before the works of his hands and fights off all the attacks of his opponent. Paul asks for deliverance from evil, remembering the things that he has already told the community. The false wonders and the great deeds of the Evil One can so affect the believer that he might succumb to him. Hence

Paul must always be concerned in his prayer that Satan does not break into the community.

Looking to the future, Paul is able to say that the Lord will continue to strengthen and preserve his community. The Lord's assistance is not limited to a particular difficult situation, as perhaps exists at that moment. The church may always hope for constant support. The Lord is faithful in all times and situations in which the church finds itself. If his people remain at his side, then the church is able to overcome all attacks against it. Paul is able to say that to the community in the power of the Lord. Thus the Lord always speaks to the church through his witnesses and comforts them.

And we have confidence in the Lord about you, that you are doing and will do the things which we command.

Paul ends his thanksgiving and his encouragement with a confident request and a blessing. At the same time he wants to make a transition to the last great argument of the letter, in which he has to admonish and exhort. He seeks to point to the model of God and Christ, so that the community can recognize in love and patience the abuses within it and remove them. Paul wants to create a wide area of openness in the hearts of the faithful so that they are capable of not rejecting immediately the stern points that he has to make.

Before Paul broaches this ticklish subject, he wants to prepare a good atmosphere for his exhortations. He is not quarreling with them but making a criticism in love in order to help the whole community. He knows that he can trust the community, because he is the father of it. They have accepted his gospel, and through it he has opened up for them fellowship with Christ.

Now he also has the right to guide the further life of the community and to correct it where it is necessary.

Although Paul is the servant of the community and seeks their confidence in a brotherly way, he is also entitled to expect obedience. As the preacher of the gospel of salvation, he must also supervise its realization in the life of the individual and of the various churches. Often enough false doctrines and a decline of faith are observed first in life, and not in teachings and words. A man who has truly accepted faith must remain faithful to the word of life, now and in the future. To live in faith means to accept readily a responsibility.

The pastor of the community must be able to expect that the members of the community will be ready to keep the obligations that they have entered into. Their life is no longer at their own disposal, but they place it at the disposal of the Lord. Through this they receive joy, freedom, and salvation. In the order of salvation a transvaluation of all values has come about: " He who loves his life loses it, and he who hates his life in this world will keep it for eternal life. If any one serves me, he must follow me; and where I am, there shall my servant be also " (Jn. 12 : 25f.).

"May the Lord direct your hearts to the love of God and to the steadfastness of Christ.

In solemn words that are reminiscent of the Old Testament, Paul prays for the community. The Lord directs and guides the hearts of men. As the creator of all hearts, he is able to guide them correctly. The goal of this guidance by God is an ever deeper knowledge of him and fellowship with Christ.

Confident of this, Paul prays for the love of God. We received his love at baptism once and for all, " because God's love has been poured into our hearts through the Holy Spirit which has been given to us " (Rom. 5 : 5). Now we are a temple of the Holy Spirit. But he prays that this reality of faith may always be seen in the community. The faithful must open their eyes and prepare their hearts to be able to recognize the constant working of God's love. The generous love of the Father has its climax in the sacrifice of his Son. " For God so loved the world that he gave his only Son, that whoever believes in him should not perish but have eternal life " (Jn. 3 : 16). Paul has experienced this fullness of the love of God. In his power he does his work. He desires to bring all men to the knowledge of the love of God. Thus he is overjoyed to see the working of God in history, and from his saving deeds he draws the consequence: " What then shall we say to this? If God is for us, who is against us? He who did not spare his own Son but gave him up for us all, will he not also give us all things with him?" (Rom. 8 : 31).

But Paul also prays that we are made capable in the Holy Spirit of loving the Father. Whoever has received the love of God can only respond with love. Love of God is automatic for someone who knows that he has received the rich present of the love of the Father. Whoever opens himself to the call of the Father in Christ loves God and is loved by him.

The second part of the prayer is directed quite specifically to the particular situation in which the community finds itself. Some impatient members have brought disquiet to the whole community. They have produced a wave of hysterical emotion at the idea that Christ was now coming very soon. Their basic failing is their impatience. They do not want to accept the sufferings of pilgrims and strangers in a world that hates God. Thus their expectation of Christ is colored by human impatience. They are working out dates and cause unrest.

Christ was not impatient in his earthly life. He taught the apostles and the people patiently. He accepted persecution, suffering, and the cross. The Father had foreordained his hour, so he did not seek to anticipate it. He said: " My hour has not yet come " (Jn. 2:4). When he entered into his passion, he was following the will of the Father: " Father, the hour has come; glorify thy Son that thy Son may glorify thee . . ." (Jn. 17:1). To follow Christ also means to await with patience and perseverance the hour which the Father has set for everyone. This is required by the readiness to fulfill the will of the Father here and now, moment by moment. The community needs to have an attitude of patience now, in this moment when the letter is read. Paul will have to attack abuses. The Lord himself, whose life of patience was intended as an example for us, is now able to make the community capable of taking this reprimand. The brethren are in a living communion with Christ. From this communion with the Lord his people receive all the gifts by means of which he guides their hearts. At the moment the impatient ones need most urgently the gift of Christ's patience.

Idleness and Laziness in the Community (3:6–16)

Paul has endeavored to prepare the community for a serious correction. Now he states what is wrong, without beating about the bush. He begins with a command. The brethren are to keep away from all idlers in the community (3:6). Paul can point to his own example. He did not let himself be supported by others but worked himself when he was in Thessalonica (3:7f.). By this he wanted to give the community an explicit example for their life (3:9). The duty to work is a part of Christian life. To lapse into laziness is a grave failing (3:10). Thus Paul has to remind the idlers again quite firmly of their duty to work (3:11f.). He follows this exhortation with a number of instructions for the whole community. The community should not slacken in love. If someone is not ready to alter his life, then he must be excluded from the community. But he still remains for the faithful a brother, so that he must not be despised in a spirit of unchristian pride (3:13–15). The prayer for peace (3:16) is intended to keep alive and preserve understanding and goodwill in the community.

Idle Fellow Christians Should Be Shunned (3 : 6)

⁶*Now we command you, brethren, in the name of our Lord Jesus Christ, that you keep away from any brother who is living in idleness and not in accord with the tradition that you received from us.*

Paul commands in the name of the Lord Jesus Christ. The Lord and his Apostle make up a living unity. It is with authority that Paul passes judgment on the abuses that have arisen. It is from the Lord that he received the command that he has to pass on to the community. Thus the community must obey. The Apostle has an official authority. With this authority he can issue commands to men who seek to live in obedience towards God. If the man reprimanded accepts the order with humility and changes his behavior, this proves the genuineness of his faith. But the Apostle never becomes arrogant. He never forgets for a moment that they are all brethren beloved of the Lord. Thus even here, where he is forced to make use of his official authority, he addresses the faithful with the affectionate term " brethren."

It is with obvious emotion that Paul forbids the community to have anything to do with the idlers. They do nothing but kill time. Perhaps these lazy brethren have even let themselves be supported by the community, by going everywhere where there was something to be had for nothing. This can be a source of irritation to well-meaning Christians, who are happy to serve their neighbor.

But Paul sees even the idlers as brethren. Even those who fall short are brethren beloved by the Lord. They belong to the great community of Christ. So the attitude which Christians ought to have to those who have fallen short in the community is not to be a superior, loveless one. Nevertheless, Paul gives exact instructions about what is to be done with these people. They are to be avoided so that they might reflect. It is not so much a punitive measure as an educational one. By being temporarily excluded from the community, the disobedient ones are to be urged to reflect and improve.

Laziness in a Christian community is particularly serious. It is part of Paul's fundamental preaching that every man is quietly to go about his work. This is intended to counter the widespread arrogant view that work is something only for slaves. It is not a disgrace to help to transform the world and to earn one's daily bread, but a fulfillment of God's creation. Thus the idlers are in open opposition to the apostolic tradition. During his stay in Thessalonica, Paul emphasized the preaching of this point by his own example. " For you remember our labor and toil, brethren; we worked night and day, that we might not burden any of you, while we preached to you the gospel of God " (1 Thess. 2:9). Paul is able, therefore, to remind them in the following of his own example.

The Apostolic Example (3 : 7–9)

[7]*For you yourselves know how you ought to imitate us; we were*

not idle when we were with you, ⁸we did not eat anyone's bread
without paying, but with toil and labor we worked night and
day, that we might not burden any of you.

Paul justifies his strict command with a reproach. This kind of
abuse should not have occurred in Thessalonica. He had shown
them clearly enough how a Christian should live his everyday
life. And he had not only lived a model life in their town, but
also explained to them his way of life. Paul notes with dis-
appointment that it was particularly in Thessalonica that he did
everything in order to give the community an example of a
Christian life, and still they have failed.

When Paul was in their town, he had consciously refused all
support. The teaching of Christ was to be proclaimed purely and
clearly. Paul did not want to give the impression that he wanted
to draw personal gain from the proclamation of the gospel of
salvation. He had not been idle. He had paid the families who
had taken him in for looking after him, down to the last penny.
In this way the Thessalonians were able to see his purity of
motive. They cannot reproach him with what Paul had to say of
other preachers of the good news: " Some indeed preach Christ
from envy and rivalry . . . the former proclaim Christ out of
partisanship, not sincerely but thinking to afflict me in my
imprisonment " (Phil. 1 : 15.17).

The trade of a tentmaker, which Paul pursued in Corinth,
involves much toil and labor. It needs a great deal of strength of
will and self-sacrifice to do this heavy work. A free Greek regarded physical labor as incompatible with his dignity as a man.
Menial tasks were to be performed by slaves. A Christian, however, is not ashamed of his work, for in it he confesses God the
creator, whose whole work of creation is good. Hence it would

be to fall back into paganism to reject the toil and labor of work and regard idleness as a life worthy of a free man. In his Greek environment it was necessary for Paul to counter the mistaken view that he was only a new teacher of wisdom who expected to be paid well by his pupils.

But Paul earned his own living, out of discreet thoughtfulness for others. The majority of Christians in Thessalonica were poor, and had to toil and labor to support themselves. Any additional claim on them would have been a burden and would have increased their difficulties. Paul's sensitivity differs agreeably from the idler's consideration. This openness is due to his generous love. Love even does without things that it could lay claim to, and is a quiet but effective protest against all selfishness, which does not hesitate to make demands even where it is obviously in the wrong.

Paul wants to show here that work is also a form of realization of Christian love of one's neighbor. A man who goes quietly about his onerous and monotonous daily work does not need to trouble other people. As he is thrifty and modest in his needs, he is also able to help where there is real distress, " for God loves the cheerful giver " (2 Cor. 9:7). But it is outrageous for people—perhaps even from pious motives—to be a burden to the Christians who work away quietly.

⁹It was not because we do not have that right, but to give you in our conduct an example to imitate.

After explaining his behavior in the community, Paul considers the principle of the thing. It is not automatic that the preacher of the gospel should also do manual labor. Rather, he should be free to preach the gospel. Hence the community

should support him. Christ himself had given this instruction to
his disciples: " And remain in the same house, eating and
drinking what they provide, for the laborer deserves his wages "
(Lk. 10:7). Paul gave up a right to which he could lay claim
when he worked in Thessalonica. The good pastor was concerned
to be a model for his flock. He did not assert his right, but by
his behavior gave the community an example of what everyday
Christian life should be in the world. As a worker among
workers, he hoped that he would have better success with simple
working men. Witnesses to Christ give up their rights if it
means that Christ can be preached in a better and clearer way.
In a different situation Paul will very clearly point out the fact
that the apostle is also working when he preaches the gospel of
salvation. Therefore, he rightly deserves wages also. " Do you
not know that those who are employed in the temple service get
their food from the temple, and those who serve at the altar
share in the sacrificial offerings? In the same way, the Lord
commanded that those who proclaim the gospel should get their
living by the gospel " (1 Cor. 9:13f.).

A Reminder of an Earlier Exhortation
Concerning Idleness (3:10–12)

[10]*For even when we were with you, we gave you this command:*
If any one will not work, let him not eat. [11]*For we hear that*
some of you are living in idleness, mere busybodies, not doing
any work. [12]*Now such persons we command and exhort in the*
Lord Jesus Christ to do their work in quietness and to earn their
own living.

When Paul was preaching in Thessalonica, he had also spoken about the Christian relation to work. One of his teachings, which the Thessalonians must still have remembered clearly, was: if anyone will not work, let him not eat. This statement was already well known as a proverbial piece of human wisdom. The will to work and the right to support belong together. If, therefore, someone does not want to work, he is to get nothing to eat. Through this instructive measure he will soon be forced to earn something. The new gospel does not remove fundamental and obvious insights of human life together. The Lord came into this world as we have it. He did not want to take his people out of the world and prescribe for them an existence remote from it. Christianity is realized in everyday life.

Concerning life in the community, Paul had heard that a few idlers were irritating the faithful and causing unrest in the life of the community. They were killing time and achieving nothing. At the moment it was only a few who live in this way; but a few men who give a bad example could very quickly infect the whole community. This is also true within a Christian community. These good-for-nothings turned up here and there and perhaps interfered in things that had nothing to do with them. From time to time they did something if they felt like it. They no longer engaged in any hard work and looked for easy occupations. So they hung about and disturbed the peaceful life of the community because they irritated the brethren.

It is not quite clear why these people had fallen into this lazy way of life. It may be that they had again adopted their pagan ways, arrogantly despising manual labor. But they may also have given up their work because of the fantastic notions held concerning the imminent coming of the Lord. If the Lord is coming in any case within the immediate future, what is the

point of going on working? This is the way they may have
thought and may even have considered themselves, because of
this opinion, more pious and believing than others who, despite
the rumors about the appearance of the Lord, continued to work
in the same way as before. Extravagant religious emotion and
laziness go well together.

Paul had to take energetic steps so that no false ideas sprang
up about Christian life in the community and the surrounding
environment. Faulty manifestations of Christian life could
greatly hinder the preaching of the truth. Therefore, by the
power of his authority in the name of the Lord Jesus Christ he
gave strict instructions to the idlers. He was not speaking to the
community. These idlers must be named directly. He wanted to
remind them of their duty to work.

Even here where Paul had to be very strict, he did not forget
that the church must always and in every situation be a brotherhood. There must never be a hard and unbending judgment in
the church. This is why he followed his instruction immediately
by a fatherly exhortation. They were not only to obey his command, but to accept consciously and voluntarily his exhortation.
Their father and brother commanded and exhorted in the Lord
Jesus Christ.

Paul's exhortation is very concrete. They are to live sensibly
and work well. Only in this way will their life become ordered
again. They will be content with themselves and the world. A
man who works quietly places himself responsibly and humbly
within human society. He does not ask for special treatment and
privileges. In this way he contributes to a peaceful development
of society and community life. A quiet, peaceful, and ordered
life is also the best foundation for a lively and sound faith. Paul
asked his helper Timothy to make intercession for all those in

responsible places that this peaceful life be guaranteed: " First of all, then, I urge that supplications, prayers, intercessions, and thanksgivings be made for all men, for kings and all who are in high positions, that we may lead a quiet and peaceable life, godly and respectful in every way. This is good, and it is acceptable in the sight of God our Saviour . . ." (1 Tim. 2 : 1–3).

Then the idlers, who are now living on other people, no longer need to be a burden on others. They are able to live contented on what they earn themselves. Christian love of one's neighbor is based on justice. People who are too lazy to work, but appeal to Christian love of one's neighbor in order to be supported offend against justice. Everyone has the right and the duty to eat the bread that he has earned himself. In this way the brethren are then able to live together in harmony.

Some Instructions for the Whole Community (3 : 13–15)

¹³*Brethren, do not be weary in well-doing.*

Now the whole community is addressed again. Paul had to discuss fundamental questions in connection with the abuses that had arisen. He had clearly branded as wrong the behavior of some members of the community. Paul hoped that those concerned would reflect and find their way back to a sensible life. It may be, however, that people were beginning to feel bitter in the community. Perhaps some had already said that they had been exploited by these idlers. Now Paul has agreed with them. So they might consider themselves confirmed in their view and withdraw from helping people. They had made the unhappy discovery that Christian love of one's neighbor is not possible.

One does a good work in faith in the Lord Jesus Christ. Others see your goodwill and exploit you. The consequence of this insight could now be that there is no point in doing good. Through disappointments good Christians might weary of love of their neighbor. But then the community would lose its radiating power. Thus Paul must warn the good ones against resignation.

If the idlers are in difficulties because of their wrong attitude, then the community will have to continue to help them until they can again manage on their own. The community should not refuse them this support if they see the goodwill of those who have been reprimanded. It is just in the time of conversion that the selfless love of the disciple of Christ should help converts without regard for their past sins. The convert is gladdened by this openness, and conversion is made easier for him. This goodness and generosity finds its model in the attitude of the Lord himself, who said: " Those who are well have no need of the physician, but those who are sick. Go and learn what this means: ' I desire mercy, and not sacrifice.' For I came not to call the righteous, but sinners " (Mt. 9 : 12f.).

14If anyone refuses to obey what we say in this letter, note that man, and have nothing to do with him, that he may be ashamed.

It may be that some idlers may not listen to the exhortations that Paul has given in this letter. That cannot just be accepted. The life of the whole community depends on the behavior of these people, and that is why Paul's instructions must be obeyed. He must prescribe disciplinary measures. Since the idlers disturb the life of the community, they must be kept apart from the community until they change their attitude.

But these refractory members of the community must not be abandoned by the Christians. The simplest solution would be to dismiss the idlers out of weakness or anger and continue the life of the community. But the whole community is responsible for all Christians, even for one's unattractive fellow citizens. Paul states how the community is to behave with the refractory brethren. These people should be made known. The community is to know who refuses to obey Paul's instructions. They are injuring the life of the community and therefore should not remain unknown. It is also important for the charity work of the community to know who is unnecessarily demanding support. Those who damage the life of the community must experience the fact that their behavior is damaging to themselves also.

An important educative measure is also exclusion from the love-feast of the community. Everyone should contribute something to this love-feast, according to his capacities. Probably the idlers always appeared punctually without bringing anything. This has irritated the other Christians. To exclude them from the love-feast is a good way of shaming the guilty ones. It will be painful for them to want to take part in the common meal but to be rejected because they cannot contribute anything that they have earned themselves. If they are shamed in this way, then perhaps they will be able to bring to the next gathering something of the fruits of their own work, which they have taken up again.

15*Do not look on him as an enemy, but warn him as a brother.*

Despite all exhortations and punishment the faithful must not forget that they must still remain the brethren of those brethren who fall short. The community may on no account overstep the borders set by God's will. A Christian who falls short has still been received into the community through faith and baptism. Disharmony in the community could lead to unchristian quarreling. That would be the end of efforts to establish a good and sound community life. Human emotions and primitive hate can lead to actions that are unfitting for redeemed men. A terrible reversal of fronts could also take place. If the " just men " despised and hated the idlers, as one does in the case of an enemy, then their guilt would be far greater than that of the idlers. An offense against fraternal love is worse than the sin of the idlers. Men who provoke hate and enmity in a community are traitors to the redemptive work of Christ. They must then be reminded of the words of the Lord: " How can you say to your brother: ' Let me take the speck out of your eye,' when there is a log in your own eye? You hypocrite, first take the log out of your own eye, and then you will see clearly to take the speck out of your brother's eye " (Mt. 7 : 4ff.).

A Prayer for Peace (3 : 16)

[16]*Now may the Lord of peace himself give you peace at all times in all ways. The Lord be with you all.*

With a prayer for peace Paul concludes what he has to say about the idlers. He is not concerned with being right or enforcing his own opinion. He wants to open men's hearts to the peace that only God can grant. But true peace comes only to the men and the community that are open to God and his saving work. So may God give the community this peace " at all times in all ways." As the creator and preserver, God can instruct men in the right way of life; that is why he is the Lord of peace who alone can give peace. His Son Jesus Christ, as the one sent by the Father, has made final peace with our world. A man who places himself under the cross of Christ and experiences and takes into himself its saving power can live in this world already in perfect peace. " For he is our peace, who has made us both one, and has broken down the dividing wall of hostility by abolishing in his flesh the law of commandments and ordinances, that he might create in himself one new man in place of the two, so making peace, and might reconcile us both to God in one body through the cross, thereby bringing the hostility to an end " (Eph. 2 : 14–16).

Paul's attacks against those who disturb the peace are intended only to serve the peace of the community. It is important that the community should realize his intention. Thus, as a loving pastor, he wants to show his pure motives by concluding his exhortations and instructions by wishing them peace.

Paul is coming to the end of his letter. He greets the whole community with the Christian greeting that is at the same time also a prayer. In the community assembled for the worship of God the Lord is present in a special way. Here his gospel is proclaimed again through the mouths of the apostles and disciples; here he can again appear as Lord and teacher. At the beginning of his letter Paul had stated clearly that the Lord is present in his community. This is the first time in the New Testament that this greeting " The Lord be with you " is written down. It was undoubtedly already customary in the community—at any rate in the liturgy—and will remain through all the centuries an essential part of Christian worship.

In a special addition Paul realizes that which he has commanded the community. Even the idlers continue to belong to the community; they are and remain brethren. Thus Paul wishes that the Lord may remain with them all, with the good and zealous, but also with the idlers and those who fall short. When it is a question of salvation of men, the prayer must include everybody, without distinction of person or moral achievement.

THE CLOSE OF THE LETTER
(3:17–18)

THE CLOSE OF THE LETTER (3:17-18)

Paul's Greeting in His Own Handwriting (3:17)

17I, Paul, write this greeting with my own hand. This is the mark in every letter of mine; it is the way I write.

Paul dictated his letters. This is the reason for the fact that the style is sometimes uneven. Of course, his letters are inspired with such great urgency that the established grammatical forms cannot contain the full richness of his ideas. In Paul's letters we can often share in his wrestling for the right answers. Through his personal signature Paul seeks to confirm that the letter is a genuine one, but he is also adding a fraternal greeting. To the very last line the letter is illuminated by the basic attitude of brotherly love. Paul, the pastor, the father, the brother, loves his communities and the brethren and sisters, who live, like him, " in the Lord."

But here the personal signature of the Apostle fulfills an especially important purpose. There seem to be people who are circulating forged letters by Paul. By this means they are gaining recognition among the Christian communities for their false teachings. But these dealings are bringing Paul into bad repute. That is why he must emphasize that this is the way he writes. This is what his signature looks like. Other signatures betray the forger and should be rejected by the community. The community must be especially on its guard in the struggle against " false brethren " (2 Cor. 11:26), who seek to spread a watered-down or exaggerated Christianity which is not in accordance with the apostolic tradition. Paul has received revelation; he can validly proclaim the gospel. A man who says anything different is a deceiver. " Not that there is another gospel, but there are some who trouble you and want to pervert the gospel of Christ. But even if we, or an angel from heaven, should preach to you a gospel contrary to that which we preach to you, let him be accursed " (Gal. 1 : 7f.).

The Grace (3 : 18)

¹⁸*The grace of our Lord Jesus Christ be with you all.*

Paul's pastoral letter to one of the oldest Christian communities in Europe ends with a brotherly blessing. He began his letter with this greeting, and he ends it with it. Throughout all the ages the church wishes itself this. After all, our whole life depends on the grace of our Lord Jesus Christ. Without Christ we can do nothing. He guides, directs, and strengthens us in all the situations of this world's pilgrimage. His grace comforts us in all the suffering that we have to undergo from our oppressors. Through the grace of the Lord we will one day be gathered with him and freed from the coming judgment of wrath. But the grace of the Lord also constantly directs the community to the right path, strengthens the faithful, and leads sinners to repentance. It alone can grant true peace to human hearts. Thus everywhere the power and fullness of the Lord is at work.

Once again Paul makes the point that grace is to be with all the brethren and sisters. Through his brotherly greeting he wants to avoid any suggestions that he had reprimanded anyone in human anger. He was only concerned with opening the door to the grace of the Lord.